Woof!

Woof!

The
Funny
and Fabulous
Trials
and
Tribulations
of 25 Years
as a Dog Trainer

Matthew Margolis
with
Mordecai Siegal

Crown Trade Paperbacks
New York

Photograph credits: Page 4, 17 (top left and bottom left), and 55: Helene Steel. Page 5, 6, 9, 17 (top right), 22, 60, 94, 108, 170, 177, 198, 203, and 210: Mordecai Siegal. Page 34, 58, 117, 122, and 150: Mark Handler. Page 192 and 193: Yvette Roman.

Published by Crown Trade Paperbacks, 201 East 50th Street, New York, New York 10022. Member of the Crown Publishing Group.

Originally published in hardcover by Crown Publishers, Inc. in 1994. First paperback edition printed in 1995.

Random House, Inc. New York, Toronto, London, Sydney, Auckland

CROWN TRADE PAPERBACKS and colophon are trademarks of Crown Publishers, Inc.

Manufactured in the United States of America

Design by Linda Kocur

Library of Congress Cataloging-in-Publication Data
Margolis, Matthew.
Woof!: the funny and fabulous trials and tribulations of 25 years as a dog trainer/by Matthew Margolis with Mordecai Siegal–1st ed.
p. cm.
1. Margolis, Matthew. 2. Dog trainers–United States–Biography.
I. Siegal, Mordecai. II. Title.
SF422.82.M37A3 1994
636.7'0887'092–dc20   93–40002
                                                                              CIP

ISBN 0-517-88451-8

10 9 8 7 6 5 4 3

For Beverly

contents

foreword

viii

preface

ix

chapter one

chicken soup

1

chapter two

park avenue

23

chapter three

heigh ho silver
(and other wonder dogs)

33

chapter four

tails from the crypt

59

chapter five

to train or not to train

78

chapter six

the write way to train

97

chapter seven

heeeeeere's matty!

119

chapter eight

the grand tour

144

chapter nine

going west

159

chapter ten

the L.A. story

178

acknowledgments

212

foreword

Writing a book in the first-person singular voice of Matthew Margolis was the most delicious fun I have ever had as a writer. Each morning, for a year, I would place my fingers on the keypad and transform myself into a fireball of energy and enthusiasm that I have come to know and love for so many years. Although we have very different temperaments and metabolisms there is much common ground between us. I could not have written this book as I have if I, too, hadn't experienced the same desperate passion to be somebody doing something that was worthwhile and meaningful.

Over the years I have written many things, from veterinary medical reference books to screenplays, but working on *Woof!* was different. It was more like acting than writing. Pretending to be my dynamic friend and coauthor for five hours a day was heady stuff even if I did run the risk of an identity crisis. There were days when I wasn't sure who I was.

What appealed to me most was writing about a man who took control of his own life and molded it into something quite exceptional. Almost every dog he meets falls in love with him. Now that's animal magnetism. You can't teach it and you can't get a degree for it. His skills and talents are inborn and self-developed.

Matthew focused his life's work on his great love for dogs while overcoming many obstacles. He is a man who created himself and I admire him very much. Writing the last page was the only unhappy moment for me. I didn't want the experience to end.

MORDECAI SIEGAL

preface

Writing this book, for me, was a journey. It allowed me to go back in time and relive many of the events that have shaped my life. There were so many moments that seemed like disasters at the time that later proved to be victories, and some victories that were definitely disasters. It's been a journey crammed with laughter, a little hysteria, some anxiety, and a lot of love.

Like most people growing up, my greatest fear was trying to decide what to do with my life. It was a question that became unbearable at a time when I was truly lost and couldn't figure out where to go or what to do when I got there. Without knowing it at the time, I went down one of the many roads lined with yellow bricks, which eventually led to a happy place.

I love what I do, every day of my life. I help dogs, help people, and know that I make a difference in their lives. They help me as well. It is not an exaggeration to say that dogs have saved my life.

I'll never forget the struggle or the risks I took to get where I am. But I'll also never forget the people who were so kind and generous to help me get here.

I can't thank Mordecai enough for making this book happen. That poor man had to listen to my voice on hundreds of hours of tape and then try to be me. It was an impossible job, but he did it.

chapter one

chicken soup

We were in the reception area with a dozen people standing around but it didn't matter. She bawled like a baby as her husband and daughter tried to comfort her. All I could do was hand her tissues, one by one, and wait for her to pull herself together. There was no point in pulling any punches. There was no way to soften the news. She had to be told the truth. If I had known she was going to take it this hard I would have discussed it in the privacy of my office.

The twelve-year-old daughter handled the situation better. She held her mother's hand and gently rubbed it. The husband put his arms around his wife, patted her back, and sneaked an angry look at me. With her face buried in his shoulder he asked, "Are you sure this is necessary?"

I nodded. "I'm sure."

"But Hamlet only growled when he went under the bed. He's just a puppy."

The woman's face rose from her husband's shoulder and she sobbed even louder. "It wasn't even a growl. It was just a *Grrr Grrr*. It could've been gas."

"I don't think so," I said in a comforting tone that would have made a funeral director proud. "There's not much difference between *Grrr Grrr* and a growl. Didn't you tell me he doesn't let you go near his food without growling?"

"Yes."

"You forgot about that. Look, sooner or later he's gonna bite and you've got a kid in the house." She looked at me and for a minute I thought I had her convinced, but she threw her head back into her husband's shoulder and began sobbing again. Clients and office staff stared at us. I was getting uncomfortable.

"Would you like some coffee?" whispered my receptionist in her best understanding tone.

The weeping woman shook her head no, paused, and then reached out and grabbed her by the arm as she tried to walk away. "I'll have a bagel," she said tearfully, without looking up. She clutched the receptionist by the arm again, pulling her back. "With a shmear of cream cheese."

"Right," said the receptionist.

"And a Danish, with walnuts on it."

"You bet," said the young woman as she freed her arm and walked away. The other woman's head popped up from her husband's shoulder. "Make it a *big* shmear of cream cheese," she said as she looked around the room to see who was listening. "It's the puppy. I've put two inches on my hips since we got him. I never knew dogs were fattening."

"Neither did I. Well, look. You've got to decide," I said. "If you want the problem solved you'll have to leave him here for at least six weeks."

"Oh, God," she moaned.

I put my arms around the couple's shoulders and gently maneuvered them down the hall and into my office. "Make yourselves comfortable and talk it over. I'll be back." I closed

Dogs are love covered with fur. They're irresistible.

the door, rubbed my forehead, and took three aspirins. The receptionist returned with a tray of bagels and coffee. As she opened the door I could hear the husband say through his clenched teeth, "Leave the goddamn dog here or take the goddamn dog home. Just make up your mind, will you?"

It was combat as the woman shot back, "Not six weeks!" The door closed again.

I live through these scenes five days a week. Some are really off the wall. But I don't mind. Dogs and the people who love them get to me. They can be so touching and irritating at the same time. One thing for sure, they are never boring.

By the time my clients come to me they are no longer casual. When they first get a dog it starts out as a fun thing, like buying the latest ice cube crusher–TV combination. But one lick on the cheek and the dog transforms instantly from

*By the time my clients come to me they are no longer casual.
People with dog problems come to me for help.*

a furry gadget to a member of the family. Suddenly he becomes a relative. Give him a bathrobe and the last of the Häagen Daz and he could be your brother-in-law. Dogs are love covered with fur. They're irresistible. But love is not blind when you live with a dog. Not if you step in their mistakes.

People with dog problems come to me for help. They are usually upset and confused. Sometimes I'm the dog's last chance, although most of their problems are solvable. I ask them to leave their dogs with me for a while so we can train them and get rid of their unacceptable behavior. It gets emotional because some people just can't bear to part with them, not even for a day. Training dogs is the easy part. If you're interested in the hard part, then pay me a visit any Saturday. It's a circus.

Saturday begins peacefully enough with a drive from my house to the bakery in Beverly Hills where I pick up a couple of huge bags of warm bagels and rolls, cream cheese, pastries, and fresh ground coffee with vanilla in it. The aroma of coffee beans and hot bakery rolls makes my mouth water and gets to people in other cars when I stop for a traffic light. You can see their noses turn in my direction.

It's a thirty-minute drive to Monterey Park and I always feel a twinge of excitement before pulling in. It's going to be another Saturday with a lot of crazy people and their dogs. But the dog's the thing. It's why I'm there.

Most of the trainers, kennel workers, and office staff were outside, milling around quietly as I pulled into the driveway.

The lull before the storm.

Their early chores were done. They were in a holding pattern, waiting for things to get busy. One or two smoked cigarettes. Some sipped coffee. Others just stared across the road.

I parked in front of the building and handed the bags of goodies to the office staff. They got the coffee started, sliced the rolls, and carefully arranged the food on large trays. I try to make it festive for the visiting dog owners with a nice spread. One or two of my former clients keep showing up on Saturdays even though their dogs haven't been there for months. Maybe it's the food. There's never a crumb left at the end of the day. Or maybe it's the people and the dogs. I sincerely doubt it's the scenery.

There is a huge cemetery across the road from the kennel with large green fields, rolling hills, gentle slopes, and beautifully manicured grass providing the nicest view in the neigh-

Time to walk the dogs and get them ready for their visitors.

borhood. Too bad it's a cemetery. It's a busy place. There are always backhoes in sight digging rectangles into the ground with their metal jaws. All day long a steady stream of cars drive through the gates. I only mention this because some of them drive into my lot after leaving the cemetery and then become clients. I think the thought of dogs cheers them up.

On this particular Saturday the trainers were quietly swapping dog stories. Hamlet and his family were already waiting for me, without an appointment. They just drove in behind a funeral procession. Across the road I could hear the engines of the backhoes. It was the lull before the storm. The only busy activity on my side of the road was in the grooming area to the rear of the main kennel building. Inside, a young woman was frantically trying to get eighteen dogs slicked up for their owners. They were coming today. The dogs looked nice. They even smelled nice. Grooming dogs is hard, messy work and you haven't lived until you've bathed eighteen of them in one morning.

Past the front entrance, the kennel consists of four buildings with a maze of chain-link fences attached to them. There are 120 outdoor dog runs created by the fences that extend from the building line. Each narrow run has a little door at the wall to let the dog go in or out of the building. There are always at least a hundred dogs in the runs. It's a crazy quilt of metal fences, gates, alleys, pathways, dogs, and people. It's well designed and it works. Most important, the dogs like it.

At this point the kennel staff had already awakened the dogs, gotten them outdoors to do their morning business, cleaned up after them, fed and watered them, walked and socialized them, and even had a nice talk with them. The new dogs sensed that something different was going on. Those that had been there a while knew it was visitors' day. The Saturday circus was about to begin.

"Matt, your eight forty-five is here. He's waiting outside," said the receptionist on the intercom. I put my coffee down and walked out to the parking area in front of the building. Once the first client showed up everybody on staff scattered.

"Mr. Gonzalez, I'm Matthew. Glad you could make it."

I extended my hand to the young man, who was trying to control a German Shepherd puppy. He was straining at the leash to get to the dogs he heard barking behind the gate leading to the patio and back areas. The man could not shake hands and control the dog at the same time. Gonzalez was in his mid-twenties and wore a T-shirt and baseball cap.

A few cars drove quietly into the parking area. People got out, some with dogs, and stood around and watched us like a show. Several trainers passed us with dogs and began their obedience sessions close by. In the back you could hear a kennel worker shout, "Dog!" which meant he was walking through the patio with a dog on a leash. It helps avoid dog fights. Despite the gathering crowd I continued the evaluation.

"What's this little guy's name?"

"King," he answered nervously. "How much is this gonna cost?" By now King had peed on everything and everyone he could find and was trying to get to my right leg.

"First," I answered, "I want to see what he's like. I'm going to give the puppy a few simple tests and figure out his personality. Then I'll know what he needs and how much it'll cost you. Okay?"

He nodded. "Okay."

I took the leash from his hand and walked the dog around

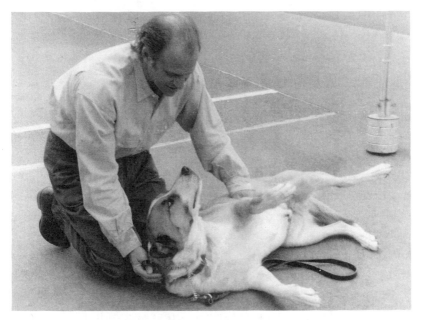

*Part of the temperament test is to roll the dog over
on his back. A dog with an even temperament doesn't mind this.*

quickly. The idea was to establish some rapport with him and
get his interest, and, if I was lucky, his trust. I called out his
name in a happy, high-pitched tone of voice. His response was
just fair so I knelt down and petted him and hugged him. He
cocked his head to one side when I whimpered like another
puppy. I knew I sounded like a goof but it worked.

The puppy became friendly so I gave him a quick lesson
for the commands Sit and Stay. His response was not good.
He would not accept my dominance. Part of the test was to
roll him over on his back and hold him in that position. He
struggled hard to get free. The young dog had no tolerance
for that position. He was a dominant-aggressive dog. Little
King began to snarl and growl. He even tried to bite me. The

woof!

man creased his brow and said, "What's going on? I've never seen him do that before."

I shook my head and said, "You've got a very aggressive dog here."

"What are you talking about? He's just a puppy. You were upsetting him."

I tried to explain. "A normal, even-tempered dog doesn't react like that."

Just then a blood-red Bronco pickup truck with four-wheel drive, high off the ground, pulled in quickly and lurched to a stop with screeching brakes. Everybody turned to see what it was. The passenger door flew open and a large Saint Bernard leaped out and hit the ground running. He barked furiously and raced all over the place like a lunatic. He tore across the training area snarling at anyone in his path. Everyone there clutched their dogs and froze with fear, including Mr. Gonzalez and his puppy. My consultation, along with the entire morning's business, had come to a complete stop.

As the big dog ran around in circles he lifted his leg and marked every corner of the lot with his urine, barking and woofing. He then galloped into the patio area, where he stood defiantly in a corner. This baby scared the hell out of everyone. His threatening posture was intimidating. A voice shouted, "Loose dog! Loose, aggressive dog."

The door on the driver's side of the Bronco opened and a gray, frizzy-haired woman in cowboy boots and jeans stepped out. She had a toothpick in her mouth and she smiled at me. The office manager ran out and whispered in my ear, "This is Mrs. Carmody. She called yesterday. She wants her dog trained." I whispered back, "Is she crazy? Why the hell did she let her dog loose?"

10

She grabbed my hand and shook it hard. "I'm Carmody. I run the Carmody Car Washes. You're Margooolis. I see your TV commercials every day. I even went out and bought your book."

"Really? Which one?"

She roared with laughter. "Which one? How the hell do I know? I didn't know you wrote more than one. What the hell can you say about dogs in two books?"

"I've written seven books." I was not happy.

She was finished discussing my literary career. "I could use some help with my big baby."

"The book didn't help your big baby?" I asked.

"I didn't read it," she said. "I just bought it to get it autographed. What can you learn from a book?"

She grabbed a book off the front seat of her truck and shoved it into my hands along with a ballpoint pen. I kept looking toward the patio as I scribbled my name on the front page. Her pen leaked and smeared ink all over my fingers. "Okay," I asked, as I handed her back her book and pen. "You've got to do something about your dog."

"Of course I do. That's why I'm here." She lowered her voice and said privately in my ear, "I been gettin' a few complaints from my neighbors. It's not really serious, though. My baby only goes after strangers."

"Yeah," I said, "but there're two hundred fifty million strangers." Some baby. I was more frightened of her than her dog. "Did you have to let him run loose like that? You were told on the phone to keep your dog in the car until I'm ready to see him."

She shook her head, spit, and said, "Well, how ya goin' to know what the *main* problem is unless you see it in action?"

11

"What's the *main* problem?"

She kicked the gravel with her boot and said, "Well, he's sorta bitten a couple of people."

"Uh-oh," I muttered. "We'd better get him on a leash right away. What's his name?"

"Rommel."

"Oh, swell," I muttered as I walked toward the Desert Fox who was holding the high ground in my patio.

I stuck out my right arm like a surgeon and someone slapped a leash and choke collar in my hand. You could almost hear the artillery rumble as I marched slowly toward Rommel. He was seated on the cement walk with his massive body backed against the wall of the building. He rose to all fours, growled and showed his teeth as I moved in. I'm not ashamed to say I was scared. This two hundred–pound monster was not Benji. I didn't want to become lunch and end up across the street with a backhoe digging me a new home. This dog was dangerous. I wiped the sweat off my brow and moved in closer. Suddenly the loudspeaker crackled and my receptionist's voice riddled the area.

"Matthew. Your nine-fifteen Akita is here. He's a leg humper." I looked at the loudspeaker and looked at the dog.

"No offense, Rommel, but I'd rather be with the leg humper." His eyes squinted and got darker. He let out another growl when I moved. A chill ran up my back and in my mind I could see him running into the cemetery with one of my legs in his mouth. There was total silence. Everyone stopped breathing and you could hear a pin drop. It was tense. I spoke softly and soothingly.

"Rommel. Oh, Rommel, what a beautiful name. Are you a good boy? Of course you are. What a good boy. Easy now.

Easy. Uncle Matty's got a present for you.'' I started to whimper like a puppy. The Desert Fox tilted his head to the side and looked at me quizzically. He was almost cute, but his curled upper lip and bared teeth sort of killed that impression.

I slowly slipped the collar over his head and brought him under control with the attached leash. You could hear everyone sigh with relief. The trainers gathered around and congratulated me. I shook my head and tried to hide my shaking hands.

Once the leash was around his neck the big dog became passive. I walked him around, put him in Sit and then Stay for a few seconds. He became very manageable. He wouldn't let me touch him, though. He was a fear-aggressive dog and was menacing because of his insecurity and anxiety. I thought about Carmody and understood his problem. She made me insecure, too. Getting him away from his own territory at home, training him, and socializing him around friendly people was exactly what he needed to build up his confidence and sweeten him up. It is what my staff does best.

I handed the leash to the gal in charge of the trainers and tried to come down from the excitement. The situation could have turned ugly at any time. She walked Rommel to a dog run in the rear of the kennel. Mrs. Carmody pushed through the small crowd and said, ''That's good stuff, Margooolis. You're better in person than on television. If we can agree on the money, you got yourself a job.''

As she turned away I pretended to reach for her throat with both hands. The small crowd applauded. ''Do it,'' they whispered. She turned around and I lowered my hands like lightning. I turned to the staff and said, ''Okay, everybody. Let's train some dogs. And, hey! Let's be careful out there.''

On my way to the reception area I darted by Mr. Gonzalez who was holding on to his puppy for dear life. As I passed him I said, "I'll be right with you. We have to talk. Let me just say hello to the leg humper." I muttered to myself, "I'd rather deal with a lover than a fighter, anyway."

The loudspeaker crackled again. "Matthew, you have calls on lines one and two and there's no decision yet about Hamlet. They're waiting for you in your office."

I walked into the reception area, leaned over the counter, and whispered, "Did you hear them say anything in there?" The receptionist shook her head no. The office door was open so I peeked in. Hamlet's mother was still crying and her husband and daughter were patting her back. I closed my eyes and took a deep breath.

Just then I felt someone's finger poke my back. "Matty. It's me."

I turned around and saw a familiar face. "Hey, how are you?" Once I realized she was pregnant I remembered who she was. She had the dog with the humping problem. "Jeanine. How's the mommy? You getting kicked around in there yet?" She was pleased that I remembered her. "Where's ah, ah . . ."

"Hirohito," she answered. "He's in the car." Tears started forming in the corners of her eyes and then slowly ran down her face.

I licked my dry lips, breathed deeply, put my arm around her, and steered her and her very large tummy to a corner of the office. It was getting jammed in there with trainers, clients, and prospective clients walking in and out, pouring coffee, smearing cream cheese on bagels, and watching my private tape on the TV monitor. It showed a segment of "The Today

Show" with Bryant Gumble interviewing me and showing my work at the kennel. I ran it on a continuous loop for my clients because it was an important example of aggressive dogs before and after training. It made it easier for people to understand what could happen with an aggressive dog. The sound was turned up. The phones were ringing and a lot of people were talking dogs at the same time. It was getting crazy.

I gently rubbed Jeanine's belly with the flat of my hand. "What's the matter, Jeanine? Is everything all right?" She was trying to hold back the tears without success. "No."

"Don't worry," I said. "We'll solve Hirohito's problem. It'll get done. When a dog humps we know what to do. I know it's upsetting . . . "

She stopped me with her hand and then blurted, "I did the math. If I leave Hiro with you today, then he won't be home when I get out of the hospital." She then started sobbing major tears. "I don't think I can bear that. I want him home with me when I get out." She began to cry. I now had two clients in tears. "It's not crazy, is it, Matty?" she asked, staring hard into my eyes.

"Yes. Yes it is," I answered with a forced smile. I reached for the tissues. The boxes were everywhere. I looked into my office out of the corner of my eyes and saw Hamlet's mother leave her husband's arms, stand up, and walk toward the door. She seemed to have found her composure, but then started to sob again. By then her husband had started crying, too. Their daughter stomped across the floor and left the room, slamming the door. She marched outside and sat down in her parents' car. Apparently she'd had it with them.

"Jeanine. Have a bagel. I'm sure the baby is hungry. I'll be right back."

I went in the office to get it over with. This situation was taking up too much of my time. "Have you made a decision for Hamlet? What's it gonna be?" Hamlet's mother said to me through a tissue, "Six weeks is too long. I can't do it. I can't leave him here for six weeks. I'll miss him too much. How am I going to fill my day?"

I said, "Ma'am, you have a daughter. Surely she needs your attention."

"That doesn't take long," she snapped. "She goes off to school early in the morning and then I'm alone for the rest of the day."

I had to end this. "I've got an idea. I'll get one of my people to take you, your husband, and your daughter on a tour of the kennel. It's an interesting place. It might help you make up your mind. If you decide to leave Hamlet, you can come here every Saturday to visit and bring him toys and yummies and play with him."

She thought about it, got up, and walked to the door. "Every Saturday? I can visit him?"

I nodded. "There are a lot of people here today doing just that. Talk to them."

"Maybe," she said thoughtfully. They left the office and took the tour with one of the kennel staff. By now several of the scheduled visitors had arrived.

The place is like a summer camp for dogs. Every Saturday, dozens of nervous, anxiety-ridden people show up loaded with gifts for their dogs. You can feel their excitement. They come each week like parents at a sleep-away in the mountains. When they get here, though, they look like they're having a nervous breakdown. It's a good thing dogs don't laugh. If you don't

The place is like a summer camp for dogs. The owners come each week like parents at a sleep-away in the mountains.

keep boxes of tissues on every table and countertop, the mascara and sunblock flow like little black rivers. With only a few exceptions, the visiting dog parents come to the kennel loaded down with such gifts as rubber pork chops that jingle, chewed-up security blankets, and enough stress for everyone. All that's missing is the chicken soup. Why are they so stressed? I guess they feel guilty about sending their dogs away for a month and a half. And the anxiety? Simple. They miss their pets. But there's more to it. A lot of these people are afraid their dogs will forget them. Can you imagine a dog forgetting a family that brings three boxes of Kentucky Fried Chicken for him? The dogs jump for joy on visiting day.

I ran back to the parking area where I'd left Mr. Gonzalez. He was sitting on a bench looking at his puppy. His dog had a glassy-eyed stare. I asked him, "Where did you get the dog?"

He looked up at me and said, "At a pet shop."

I nodded and then asked, "Do you have any children at home?" He said his wife was seven months pregnant and he got the dog to protect her. He had never owned a dog before.

"Look, Mr. Gonzalez. I could take your money and give this dog an obedience course. But he is going to be an extremely aggressive and dangerous dog to have around the house with a baby crawling on the floor. Nothing can change that no matter how well he's trained. He was born that way. It's a breeding problem and all the training in the world is not going to make me ever trust him one hundred percent with children."

The large, black puppy settled down on the man's lap with his front paws hanging over and his large tongue drooping out. He panted as his ears went up. Like a lot of Shepherd puppies, his head had not yet grown to catch up with the size of his large, beautiful ears. He was a good-looking dog.

"My advice to you, Mr. Gonzalez, is to return this dog to the place you got him, if you can. You shouldn't have him around a small child."

I could tell that he was not going to take my advice. I got up, shook his hand, and wished him luck. He was disappointed and put the pup on the ground and trotted him to his car. The man had fallen for the dog and was going to take his chances. There wasn't anything I could do about it except pray.

I needed a break so I grabbed a cup of coffee and disappeared to a quiet part of the kennel. It was way off to the side in the back, where the protection dogs are kept. As I sometimes do, I went to the last run on the line. Sitting in the shade, all the way to the back wall, was probably the largest German Shepherd you will ever see. He was also the most aggressive one. I know; I trained him. He's my favorite dog.

His name is Gerde and he is a dominant-aggressive dog, which means he's a born leader. If he were living in a pack of dogs he would keep them all in line and decide who did what and who got what. Gerde is the kind of dog that would defend what was his to the death. Despite his ferocious look and sound, he is a great dog and I love him. There is something so appealing about his manner. There isn't a shred of self-doubt in him and he would never tolerate anyone standing at his run except me. Everyone on the staff knows to stay away from him unless they're going to feed him or clean his run. And even then, they have to do it carefully.

At times, I stand outside his run and quietly talk to him. Talking to Gerde always makes me feel better. He looks at me, blinks, and then turns away. That is high praise from a dog of his stature. You don't ever want to enter a staring duel with Gerde because that would be a challenge to his dominance and get him to take a growling run at you that you'll never forget.

Gerde lives in my kennel on a permanent basis. He is one tough customer, but we've made our peace with each other. Like two warriors, we have learned to respect each other. This dog has never allowed himself to be owned by anyone. Although he lives here permanently, I treat him like visiting royalty. He's special and I'll tell you how I got him sometime, but not now. I have to get back to work.

"Take it easy, big guy."

Gerde had refreshed me and I was ready to go back to the craziness. The morning sun was getting hot and becoming a California scorcher. My skin was heating up. I looked at the dogs with envy as I walked past each one. Most of them were sleeping on the cool, wet concrete, enjoying the shade from the roofs and trees.

My kennel is on the edge of a commercial strip in Monterey Park, which is one of a dozen sunny Los Angeles suburbs. It's not much to look at from the outside, but if you go in and take a tour it's like few places you'll ever see anywhere. If you drive by real fast you'll miss it. There is an animal hospital to the left of the kennel and a flower shop to the right. The flower shop services the cemetery across the road.

My guests are big dogs, scary dogs, and little doggies. Some are sweet, some are not. They are here because they bite or chew or dig or pee all over the house. Their owners want some kind of change in their behavior. When dogs leave my place they are no longer in danger of losing their homes, at least not because of bad behavior. The kennel is a very busy place and my friends and family tell me I'm a big success.

But after twenty-five years I still ask myself how I did it. How did a kid from the streets of Queens, New York, ever learn to train dogs for a living and get to sunny California? A lot of good things have come my way. I get to be around dogs every day of my life and get paid for it. Was it luck? Fate? Something I said? I married the right woman and that's when my luck changed. We've been together for twenty-five years and we have a son in college. He's a damn good kid. All and all, it's been one hell of a time. And it's still happening. When I think about the past twenty-five years leading to the present I marvel at the whole story and know that if I can figure it all out I can share its meaning.

As I marched down the small hill from the kennel area to the main patio I saw a sight that fascinated me. There was Nellie Steinmetz, a sixty-five-year-old client who was here to visit her dog. She was sitting on a bench under a large tree holding court with a small crowd of people. Gathered around her were Jeanine with the humping Akita, and Hamlet's family, all three of them, and some of the others here to visit their dogs. Some sat next to Nellie and the rest were at her feet, on the grass, like groupies. They were hanging on her every word. The silver-haired woman had her Miniature Dachshund, Sadie, tucked lovingly under her left arm. Unnoticed, I leaned against a tree and listened.

"I know how you feel, I know, I know. Listen, my little Sadie means everything to me and I couldn't bear to leave her, either. But believe me, it's a good thing. This doggie comes home with me next week and she's going to be a little lady, aren't you, sweetheart?" She grabbed the dog's upper lip with her right hand, shook it and squeezed it, and then kissed the dog's nose. "No more hiding ca-ca under the carpet, right?" Her audience laughed.

"Believe me, whatever problems your dog has, Matthew, god bless him, will get rid of them. So, you're gonna miss the dog for a while. Who wouldn't? But isn't it better she should be a little lady when she comes home instead of a heartburn? You'll see, you'll do, you'll be, and you'll get. Trust me." They laughed again. The woman was better than chicken soup. God, I love dog owners almost as much as I love dogs. How *did* I get so lucky?

My guests are big dogs, scary dogs, and little doggies. Some are sweet, some are not. When they leave they are no longer in danger of losing their homes.

park avenue

Nineteen sixty-eight was my first year as a professional dog trainer. My wife and I lived and worked out of a small apartment on the Upper East Side of Manhattan. The business consisted of an ad in the paper and a wall phone in the kitchen, and I didn't set the world on fire that year. There were many mornings when we just sipped coffee and stared at the quiet phone. It finally did ring one morning when we stopped staring at it.

"Hello, National Institute of Dog Training. This is Matthew Margolis."

There was a soft-spoken voice at the other end. It belonged to an older woman who sounded like a character in an old English movie.

"Mr. *Margoal-lllllus?*"

"Wait a minute. I got it. Margaret Dumont, *A Night at the Opera*. Marx Brothers, 1933, right? Listen, Alan, your rich old lady routine needs work." I thought it was my ex-roommate, an actor.

The voice at the other end was confused. "Is this the *Margoal-lllllus* who trains dogs?"

An alarm went off in my brain: Mistake! Mistake! The woman didn't sound real. She was like an American pretending to be English. But who was I to criticize her? I was from Queens pretending to come from Manhattan. I wasn't sure which one of us had the accent.

"This is Mrs. Roberta Farnsworth."

"Oh. What can I do for you, Mrs. Farnsworth?"

"You were recommended to me by my cook."

"Really?"

"It's about my dog's problem . . ."

"What's his problem?"

"*Her* problem."

"Sorry, *her* problem."

"My little girl . . ."

"Your dog?"

"Yes, my dog. Look, this is very difficult to discuss on the phone. My dog has a serious problem. Do you think you can help me?"

"Probably."

"Good. I want you to come to my home right away."

"Now? Right now?"

"Yes. Can you be here by eight? It's important that you meet my husband before he leaves for his office. I live at 567 Park."

"Avenue?"

"Yes."

"*Park* Avenue?"

I was halfway into my pants and almost out the door when I said yes and hung up.

"Beverly," I whispered, "hand me the puppy leash and nylon collar. This could be the car payment."

The canopy at 567 Park Avenue was impressive. It was maroon and white and it protruded from the stone building like a theater marquee. The doorman's long military coat was also maroon and white with a gold braid cord looping down from his right shoulder and under his arm. He looked like a part of the canopy. He wore white gloves and the damnedest general's hat you ever saw with another gold braid cord spread across the top like a banana peel. I thought he was the Student Prince. I didn't know whether to bow, salute, or sing.

"What do you want here?" he asked.

"I'm here to see Mrs. Farnsworth."

"Who's calling?"

"The dog trainer."

"The what?" he asked with a sneer.

He looked at me as though I was going to dirty his gloves. I'd have gotten more respect if I was Adolf Eichmann. He lifted the phone from its brass wall panel and pressed a small mother-of-pearl button. He spoke into it in a whisper. I couldn't hear what he said.

"You can go up," he said, shaking his head with disapproval.

As I started into the lobby he raised his gloved hand to my face.

"Hold it. Use the service elevator. It's around the side of the building."

"Up yours, you Park Avenue cossack." Of course I muttered that to myself. No point in getting crazy. I was two payments behind on the car.

The service elevator stopped at the ninth floor and the operator slid the gate open without looking at me or saying a word. I was in the back end of the largest apartment I had ever seen in my life. It occupied two entire floors and consisted of twenty-one rooms. A maid greeted me and told me to follow her. If she hadn't, I'd probably still be there, wandering through the halls like Dorothy trying to get back to Kansas. She led me through more rooms and hallways than I could count. I never saw so many couches in one place before. Finally, the journey ended in a huge living room. I waded through carpeting up to my ankles. It was the most luxurious place I'd ever seen.

"Have a seat, please," said the maid.

As I sat on a satin striped couch I slowly plunged six inches into a cushion. I gazed around at the room as I continued to submerge. You could hear the air hissing out. It was like sinking into a huge jelly doughnut.

The table next to the couch had a million dollars' worth of tiny porcelain dogs on it. One wrong swipe of my elbow and I'd have been in hock for the rest of my life. I looked around the room and saw dozens of paintings and figurines of little dogs everywhere. There was a small brass dog bed on the floor with a fluffy white linen pillow in it. The linen pillowcase had a red satin bow sewn onto the corner with a four-inch lace border all around it. The bed was surrounded by several colorful balls, chew toys, squeak toys, stuffed fuzzy things, and a rack on the wall with an assortment of bejeweled collars and leashes hanging from it.

The silence was finally broken when Mrs. Farnsworth came into the room. You could hardly hear anything except the sound of her dress rubbing against her slip as she moved toward me. She was about sixty years old, thin, and a bit frail looking. But she had a kind face, and a sweet, almost shy nature. She was very dressed up for eight in the morning. Her face was made up and her hair was perfectly groomed. She was an old-time, Park Avenue lady. The real thing.

"Mr. *Margoal-lllllllus*, it was nice of you to come over here on such short notice," she said as she extended her hand to me.

I rose from the couch, shook her hand and said, "No problem. I hope I can help you."

"I hope so, too," she said as she sat down on the chair facing the couch.

"Where's your dog?"

"Upstairs." She directed her voice to a staircase across the room and called up, "Little girl. Come on. Come down to Momma."

I heard a sudden, frantic clicking sound upstairs. It was the dog's nails scraping against the parquet floor tiles as she scampered to the stairway. The dog barked and snorted with excitement as she hopped downstairs, two steps at a time, ran across the room, jumped into Mrs. Farnsworth's lap and licked the cosmetics off her face. The woman threw her head back and laughed. At that moment there were very few differences between us. She was like every dog owner I knew. It was a happy sight.

"This is my Pekingese, Poofie," she said as she cuddled the dog in her arms.

Of course. What else would she have named her dog? This was not a Fang or Warlord. It had to be Poofie. I knelt down and called to her in the high-pitched, babylike voice I usually use for dogs that I meet for the first time. It is a technique I learned early in the game to get a dog to bond with me quickly or at least get its attention. It usually works.

"Poofie, baby. Commere. Yes. I want to meet you. Come on, sweetheart. Come to Matty."

The dog leaped off the woman's lap and ran to me with a friendly little bark. She was a beauty. Her coat was a combination of sable and fawn and the hair on her long ears and chest flowed all the way to the carpet. She looked like a little lion as she put one paw on my knee. She gave my nose a quick lick of approval and then sat on her rear end, staring up at me. I was completely charmed.

"Poofie is a great dog, Mrs. Farnsworth. I can't imagine what the problem could be."

Her expression changed and she became very stressed.

"Well, I don't know how to say it." She paused to find the right words and the courage to say them. She looked up at me, then looked away with embarrassment. "She's a perfect angel in every way except one. I love this dog very much but I don't know how to deal with her one fault."

I couldn't tell what was coming. I could see the poor woman struggling and I didn't know how to make it easier for her since I didn't know what she was getting at.

"Why don't you just say it, Mrs. Farnsworth? When it comes to dogs there isn't anything I haven't seen or heard of before." I was ready for the worst.

The poor woman shook her head and almost came to tears. "You're right. I'll just say it." She paused, swallowed, and held her head high with dignity as she spoke in a soft tone of voice.

"Poofie makes chocolates in the house."

Suddenly, everything went quiet. I creased my brow and just stared at her. I think my mouth hung open but I'm not sure. That was it. That was the whole thing. This poor woman was in a state of torment because her dog crapped on the floor. I was truly in another world.

I thought I'd heard every toidy expression people used to cover up their embarrassment, but this one was the best. I'd heard *number one, number two, mistakes, accidents, ca-ca, tee-tee, ta-ta,* and *tinkle-bells.* But *chocolates* was a new one. It was elegant. Once I thought about it, I admired the expression.

Poofie sat there, following our conversation, looking at us. She had a queer look on her face. The minute she heard the word *chocolates* she got up and slowly walked to her brass bed and plopped down into it with gloom. The word depressed her.

I had to bite my lip because if I said the *C*-word I knew I'd lose it and blow the job. "You mean, the dog, ah, defecates on the floor?"

"Please, Mr. Margoal-lllllus."

"Okay, okay," I said as I tried to clear my throat. "Where would you like Poofie to make her *chocolates*?"

"Upstairs in my personal bathroom," she answered as she looked away from me. "Can you train her to go up there and do it on newspapers?"

"Of course. But it's gonna be hard for her to control herself as she travels through so many rooms and up the stairs every time she has to make chocolates. But let's give it a shot. Of course, she will need complete obedience training to make this work."

Mrs. Farnsworth led me upstairs to see the bathroom. I was pretty sure I could solve her problem. We went back to the living room and found Mr. Farnsworth standing at a table reading the morning paper. He was a tall man, dressed in a sharply pressed gray suit with polished black shoes. He was

partially bald and looked like he owned New Jersey or Gua-
temala. We were introduced and it was obvious that he was in
a hurry and didn't want any part of this. He couldn't care less
about me, the dog, or whatever was going on here.

"Mr. Margoal-lllllus is going to solve Poofie's problem,
Arnold."

He looked up from his *Wall Street Journal.*

"How much?" he asked abruptly.

His tone made me nervous. "The entire seven-week
course will be three hundred and seventy-five dollars, and that
covers the chocolate problem."

"What? Get out."

"What?"

"Your price. It's outrageous and I'm not paying it. Now
get out."

I was shocked. The man's reaction was beyond anything
reasonable. The price was fair. It was the going rate. Mrs.
Farnsworth turned red with embarrassment and motioned
with her hand for me to leave the room. She walked me to
the back door of the kitchen and apologized. The maid, the
cook, and even the elevator man, who was standing around
munching on a muffin, heard everything. I felt humiliated as
they laughed at me quietly. I couldn't tell if Mrs. Farnsworth
was aware of them or not. Probably not. She had her own
problems back in the living room.

As the elevator went down the acid in my stomach went
up. What a bunch of jerks. It was the longest elevator ride in
my life. My ears were burning red and I couldn't get out of
there fast enough. But life goes on and all wounds heal. I put
the Farnsworths out of my mind, even though my ears burned
whenever I thought about them.

Three weeks, two Poodles, and a Rottweiler had passed as I listened to a message on my answering machine. It was the unmistakable voice of Mrs. Farnsworth. She asked me to return her call.

"Mr. Margoal-lllllus, thank you for calling back. Can you ever forgive us for what happened on your last visit? I want to apologize for my husband's behavior. Try to understand that he had been up all night before you got there. His hiatus hernia was giving him trouble and he didn't mean what he said. Can you come back to train Poofie and solve her problem?"

"Well, I'll tell you, Mrs. Farnsworth. You're a nice person but under no circumstances would I even consider coming back. Your husband was so rude to me. He was very insulting and made me feel very bad. I don't want to experience anything like that again."

"Of course, you're right. But Mr. Margoal-lllllus, he's the one who asked for you."

"You're kidding. Why?"

"I'm sorry, I can't tell you. He'll kill me if I do."

"Mrs. Farnsworth, he may kill you, but I'm not coming back unless you tell me."

I had to swear to her that I would never tell him I knew about his situation. "I'll never let on I know. What happened?"

She paused and then quietly said, "He woke up late last night. He went to get his Maalox for his hiatus hernia. Well, he stumbled around in the dark and stepped into Poofie's chocolates with his bare feet. It was quite a mess and it upset him very much. He's been washing his toes all morning. He keeps yelling to get you over here right away."

31

I know it was mean, but I couldn't control my laughter. The sight of the man furiously scrubbing between his toes was too much. God is good.

Later that day I sat in the huge Farnsworth living room with a contract and a pen. Mr. Farnsworth was as pleasant as a new stick of gum.

"How are ya, Mr. Farnsworth," I said, extending my hand with confidence. He shook my hand without looking up at me and sort of grunted something. I smiled and loved every minute of it. I especially enjoyed knowing about his toes and him not knowing that I knew about his toes.

"Good morning, sir. I hope you're well today. I'm glad you changed your mind. You've made Poofie and me very happy."

In my pocket was a box of very expensive doggie chocolates that I had picked up at a pet store. I pulled it out, opened it, and offered a handful to the dog.

"Would Poofie like some chocolates? Here baby, help yourself."

The dog licked my cheek, grabbed one of the treats from my hand, took it to her brass bed, and ate it delicately. She looked up at me with her tongue hanging out and blinked. Mr. Farnsworth looked away. I winked at Poofie and, I swear, she winked back. I love that dog and I always will. And yes, I did make my car payment that month.

chapter three

heigh ho silver
(and other wonder dogs)

Before there was Beverly, before there was dog training, before
there was anything, there was Silver the Wonder Dog. It all
began with that crazy Weimaraner and his silver-gray coat and
blue-gray eyes. He was a gorgeous animal but he was also a
lunatic. Before I get into Silver's quirks, it's important to understand that I poured everything I learned about dog training
into him. He was the first dog I trained completely as a professional. I taught him on- and off-leash obedience and gave
him total protection training. He was a superb guard dog that
you could trust with your life.

Silver was the most important dog in my life. We were
alike in so many ways. Both of us were stubborn, hard-headed,
high-energy and, at times, hysterical. We wanted more of something, but damned if we knew what. At times he was the love
of my life and at other times he was the Nightmare on Elm
Street. The two of us made the transition side by side from
dog and dog lover to a pair of professionals. I learned most
of what I know about dogs and dog training by working
through our problems together. Beverly and I used to call him
Silver the Wonder Dog because his job was to impress my clients with his perfect demonstrations of dog training. He was

Silver the Wonder Dog.

a fine example of the well-trained dog. To tell the truth, though, Silver was not always up to it. Sometimes he was great and sometimes he was a disaster. We had much in common.

I got him as a pet before I became a trainer and did everything wrong with him. I eventually did everything right with him *after* I became a professional dog trainer. In the beginning I made every mistake that a pet owner can make. He was a very nervous dog with too much energy and was always running around from lack of exercise. Here was a dog that couldn't take confinement at all, and I often confined him in a small apartment in the city. The result was he destroyed everything he could get his young teeth on. My response to that was not reasonable. I yelled at him, called him all kinds of names, and said no too often without teaching him anything. I made far too many blunders with him before I knew anything about canine behavior and training. By the time I got him under control there were many behavioral consequences. Of course, Silver was already crazy when I got him at age six months and I didn't know it at the time. I just added to his craziness. He had already been in one home that had sent him back to the breeder because of his destructive chewing and uncontrollable spurts of energy. I didn't find out about that until after I'd bought him. It was through my experience with Silver that I learned you must never holler at your dog, never point your finger in anger, never make threatening gestures with a rolled up newspaper, never chase your dog under the bed or corner him, and never, never hit your dog . . . not with your hands, not with anything. I also learned the number one rule of dog training: Punishment is not teaching. I wish I had known all this when I first got that dog. Both of us would have been spared much aggravation.

By June of 1968 I was a budding dog trainer with a shaky future but Beverly and I were engaged to be married anyway. We were close to the date of the wedding and setting up our new apartment. Beverly's parents invited us to their house in New Jersey. One of their gifts was to take us on a shopping spree for all the household staples newlyweds need to get started, like aspirin, bandages, hair spray, toothpaste, cleaners, and all the other products that add up to a lot of money. I thought it was a generous, thoughtful present.

We started out in the morning with the sun blazing down on us. Of course the Volkswagen wasn't air-conditioned and it was hot as hell inside the car. Silver was standing on the back-seat doing all he could to keep his eighty pounds from falling off as our bug chugged through the Lincoln Tunnel. We were one happy little family once we got on the Jersey Turnpike and started to pick up speed. The windows were partially open and the breeze felt good. We were driving along when all of a sudden there was a horrendous odor in the car. I slowed down and we both turned around to see where the smell was coming from. There it was. The dog had produced a monu-mental dump protruding in the middle of the backseat like a newly formed volcano as he danced nervously to avoid step-ping in it. It was directly under him, between his front and back legs. He kept staring at us with those bright, startling eyes, as if it was our fault. The dog resembled Jack Palance. You have to understand; this was a housebroken dog who had never had a problem like this before.

We pulled off the road and screeched to a stop on the shoulder to clean up the mess. I didn't want Beverly's parents to see it and think I didn't know anything about dogs. Back then they'd have questioned my ability to make a living if I couldn't get my own dog under control.

I ordered Silver out of the car and placed him in a Down-Stay position. He was by temperament a nervous, hyper dog but for some reason he was worse that morning than usual. By now he was a basket case and I wanted to calm him down. For some dog reason that I still don't understand to this day, some-thing had affected his digestion. He might have been suffering from the heat or from being in New Jersey. I opened the front trunk of the car and frantically searched for something to help me clean up. There was nothing but a spare tire, a jug of brake fluid, and a neatly folded shirt that I had picked up from the laundry the day before. I always kept a spare shirt in the car in case I was going to see a prospective client.

I feverishly removed the cardboard backing from the shirt, tore it in half and used it like a scoop and a shovel to remove Silver's nasty stuff from the seat and to get the stink out of the car. My wonder dog then howled and whined until he left the Down-Stay position and took another large dump on the grass as large as the one I had just cleaned up. I couldn't figure out where it was coming from. He had eaten his normal ration that morning. We shook our heads and laughed.

We got back in the car and again set out to my future in-laws' house. Fast-moving trucks loaded the road and it was hard getting off the shoulder and back onto the highway. I found a hole in the traffic, scooted in, and began to roll again at sixty miles an hour. As I continued driving, the memory of the smell became overpowering. I suddenly realized the smell was not a memory. That rotten dog had done it again. I turned around and saw another pile on the seat. I was caught in a nightmare that kept repeating itself. It was no nightmare, though. I was trapped on the Jersey Turnpike with the Weimaraner from Hell.

It was depressing but I pulled off the road again, took the dog out of the car, and placed him in Down-Stay. Beverly pulled the release cable of the trunk and again I searched for something to clean it up with. Like a damn fool, I had thrown away the shirt cardboard. I frantically looked everywhere in the trunk but there was nothing except my freshly laundered shirt, minus the cardboard backing. I was desperate so I unfolded my almost-new shirt and unbuttoned it. With disgust and anger I slowly wrapped Silver's third nasty mound inside my clean white shirt and rolled it into a neat bundle. I then washed the smeared residue off the seat with the sleeves dipped in brake fluid and whispered good-bye to the shirt of my dreams as we drove off into the noonday sun. Did I mention that the pocket was monogrammed with my initials?

By the time we reached her parents' house we had stopped no less than four times. Silver deposited his fourth dump on the side of the road. At least he gave me some warning for that one. He whimpered like a squeeze toy. It was a good thing he did because I was out of laundry and ready to kill him.

Later that day we had an enormous lunch with Beverly's mother and father, who thought Silver was the world's most well-behaved dog. He made a good impression. We followed their car to a mall and enjoyed the pleasure of the promised shopping spree. We bought out three stores, piled all the stuff in the backseat of the Volkswagen, and left our protection-trained dog in the front seat to guard it. We walked away from the car with all the packages in it to make one more purchase and as we did I said to Silver, "Watch!" That was a command this guard dog understood. The dog was formidable and quite scary when he sprung into action. His bite could be much worse than his bark.

You guessed it. When we got back Silver was there, but the packages weren't. Someone had simply opened the door and walked off with the stuff and Silver let him do it. He must have thought that his job was to watch the car and not the stuff inside. Some wonder dog.

I don't mean to sound ungrateful. Silver was a great asset to me as a dog trainer because he really impressed people with his execution of all the obedience commands. The problem was that his nervous, high-energy temperament meant that you couldn't always count on him when it was important.

During the time Beverly and I were planning to get married I was just barely a dog trainer and we didn't have a dime between us. The idea of having a honeymoon after the wedding was just a fantasy and out of the question. Then one day I saw a large classified ad in the newspaper that said: "Interesting way couples met. Go on ABC's 'Wedding Party.' " It also said that no matter what happens on the show, you win a honeymoon. What a great deal. We would get the trip of a lifetime if I came up with a good yarn about meeting Beverly.

I called them, made an appointment with the production staff and gave them a great story.

On the evening of September 15, 1967, I had an argument with my roommate, Alan, about Silver's chewing problem and stormed out for a walk. I took the dog with me and walked all around the Upper East Side of Manhattan until I got hungry and found myself going into the flashy new disco-restaurant, Maxwell's Plum. I sat down next to a table with three young girls from New Jersey who were visiting Manhattan for the day. One of them really caught my eye. I was dying to meet her but I needed to find a novel way to introduce myself. I wanted to impress her enough to say hello. I sent my dog Silver over to her table and commanded him to grab her by the sleeve and pull her over to me. He obeyed me perfectly and the girl, whose name was Beverly, not only said hello, but eventually said yes when I asked her to marry me eight months later. That's how we met.

They went for it. I was amazed how much they went for it. It was all true, too, except for the part about Silver. He didn't exactly grab her sleeve with his teeth and pull her over to me. It was the other way around. I dragged her over to meet Silver. I wanted to impress her with my dog.

What made me nervous was their insistence on having us recreate the scene on the show. I thought they would just interview us, we'd tell our story, the audience would laugh, and honeymoon here we come. But no. They wanted me to give a short dog training demonstration with Silver. That was no problem. Then they wanted us to reenact the scene in Maxwell's Plum and show how Silver helped me meet Beverly. That was a big problem.

I had told the show's host and production staff what they wanted to hear and now I was going to have to reproduce a scene that never happened, at least not the way I told it. We were going on the show in two weeks and the prize was an all-expense paid honeymoon to San Juan, Puerto Rico. That gave me two short weeks to teach Silver a trick I wasn't sure he could learn. If he had been a Retriever I'd have had a better chance. I'd have had a better chance if he was in his right mind. This was a crazy, hyper dog that was supposed to go to Beverly on command, grab her by the sleeve with his teeth, and pull her to me.

"There isn't a chance that the dog won't do this, is there?" asked the show's producer.

"Oh, no," I answered.

"Do you think you could get him to screw it up just once before he does it right?" the producer suggested. "You know, to get a laugh."

"I'm sure I can," I said as I stared at the floor.

Man, I really wanted that honeymoon but I didn't have a clue how Silver was going to respond to all this. In the two weeks before the show I tried to teach him the trick and he seemed to get it. I'd say, "Go get Beverly," and I'd walk him over to her on-leash, place his mouth on her sleeve and try to get him to pull her away. By the second week I'd give him the command and he'd prance over to her without me, stop, turn, and look at me with a pathetic glance and then try to nudge her to me. I figured it would be good enough if he did that much. The ad said that you get the honeymoon no matter what happens. The producer said he wanted the dog to screw it up. I wasn't worried. I *knew* he could do that.

Two weeks passed and the three of us went to the ABC studio for the "Wedding Party." Beverly and I wore our best clothes and we had Silver bathed and slicked up by a professional dog groomer. He looked great and so did we. When it was our turn we all walked out on stage and sat down with the show's host, Al Hamel. He asked me to stand up and give a short demonstration of obedience training for dogs. Silver and I performed to perfection. We impressed the audience and they applauded politely. We sat down again and Beverly and I told the story of how we met. Hamel then asked if I could get Silver to demonstrate how he went over to her and pulled her to me by the sleeve. I appeared to have all the confidence in the world. In reality, I wanted to throw up. I rose from my chair and said, "Silver, go get Beverly!"

Now I don't know if it was the hot lights, the large noisy crowd in the audience, or just plain madness, but the back part of his body began to waddle from side to side like it was swinging on a hinge. The front of his body wagged instead of his tail. He looked at me and squealed or barked or howled.

41

I couldn't tell what it was. I extended my arm, pointing to my young bride, and repeated the command, "Go get Beverly!" He rose from his Sit position, looked at me with that Jack Palance look and then ran past Beverly into the wings like a lunatic, around the curtain, back out onto the stage and then leaped into the audience. Everybody roared with hysterical laughter, pointing fingers and shaking their heads. There he was, Silver the Wonder Dog, running up and down the aisles trying to figure out how to get the hell out of there. I was on my feet barking out commands like "No! Down! Stay! Please." I finally got him under control, walked him out of the studio, and kept on going, leaving Beverly, Hamel, and all of ABC behind me. It was humiliating.

We did get our honeymoon, though. They kept their word. They sent us to San Juan but the hotel was a fleabag. They put us on the top floor in a suite with a kitchen. The place was a transient hotel where people paid by the week. We were going to eat in the hotel coffee shop but the tuna sandwich came with a side order of flies. We stayed exactly one hour. All things considered, we got what we deserved. In desperation I called my father in New York and told him what had happened. As usual, he bailed us out from the goodness of his heart and checked us into the Americana Hotel and paid for everything. We had a romantic, memorable honeymoon, thanks somehow to Silver, who, by the way, stayed home. Now I know why we called him the wonder dog. We wondered what he would do next.

During the years that I trained dogs in New York I worked in many dog owners' homes, and Silver was my calling card. Because I had concentrated my efforts on him, he had become an invaluable reflection on me. On command he would Heel, Sit, Stay, Come When Called, and go into a Down-Stay, on-leash or off-leash. He would growl on command, bark on command, and even bite on command. If I told him to go through a window he would jump through. If I told him to get in the back of the car he would hop into the backseat. When I went to a prospective client's home I would *show* them what I could do for them instead of *tell* them. After I finished my demonstration with Silver there was little or no convincing necessary. Most people hired me to train their dogs after watching him in action. But there were times . . .

I often think about the morning I went to see a wealthy family in Bedford, New York, about training their dog. I knew my dog and it was just too early in the day to introduce him to anyone. Instead, I kept him in the car. The family had a beautiful, nine-month-old, white poodle that worked well with me that morning. Because everything went so smoothly the husband and wife decided that they wanted me to train their dog. I sat down with them and had some breakfast as we discussed my fee and their Poochie's housebreaking problem. They were soft-spoken, articulate people who were worried about their dog's health as well as the stains on their expensive carpets and antique floors. I told them there was not much to worry about; anyone can easily housebreak a dog if he or she knows what to do. In a short time I had them convinced that if they followed my instructions their dog would learn how to control herself and stop using the floor as a toilet.

I wanted to reassure them so I told them about Silver's old housebreaking problems as an example and boasted how I got rid of them. I pointed to him through their kitchen window. He was sitting in the car like the obedient gentleman he was. Once they became aware of his presence they insisted on meeting him.

"Nah, let him stay out there. He's resting." I had the deal closed and there was no need to bring Silver into it.

"Don't be mean. Bring him in, it's cold out there," said the wife. She was the one who was the most upset with her dog's problem. "I'd like to meet him. Besides, it's important to see how well trained the dog trainer's dog is trained."

That made me nervous. She gave me no choice. Reluctantly, I brought Silver in from the car and put on a training show that impressed them. When it was over I placed my big, goofy dog in Down-Stay on the living room carpet and went into the kitchen with the husband. We sat at the table, sipped some coffee, and discussed the contract. He was about to sign it as his wife shrieked from the living room.

"Oh, my God! Stop! Stop it!"

I ran into the room and saw Silver standing with a content expression on his face. His hind leg was up in the air as he peed quarts all over her flocked wallpaper that had been rose, mauve, and dusty green. Silver put a dark stain on their wall as big as Australia. All I could say was, "Oh, God, it's his kidney operation. That's why I left him in the car. He needs more time. He needs more time." I couldn't leave their house fast enough. Silver quietly stared out the car window on the long ride back to New York. He didn't utter a sound. Neither did I. Believe it or not, they did sign the contract and I did train their Poochie, even though Silver destroyed their wall. They loved dogs and forgave us. They thought I was very kind and tolerant to put up with such a dog. Once again, Silver somehow came through for me.

I used to train many dogs in Manhattan. When I did, Silver was always in the car with me. I could take him out and walk him off-leash anywhere because he was so well trained. Occasionally, I'd have to double-park the car in front of another parked car if I wanted to see my client. That is a fact of life for anyone doing business in Manhattan. I would double-park, give the hour lesson, and then come back. I rarely had a problem.

One afternoon I came down from my client's apartment and heard a racket going on. Some poor guy couldn't pull out because I was double-parked in front of him. He honked and cursed at someone but I couldn't figure out who he was yelling at. The man had murder in his heart as only a frustrated New York driver can. A few people stopped to watch the impending violence as he stepped out of his car with venom. It looked like someone was going to get punched. I couldn't figure out who he was yelling at.

"Move your goddamn car, or so help me I'm gonna put your lights out."

I realized he was shaking his fist at someone sitting in the front seat of my car. He must have broken in to steal it. As I rushed to the scene I almost fell to the ground in laughter. There was Silver, sitting up at the wheel in the driver's seat. He had managed to wrap himself up in my coat, with the collar up, and he looked like a man, sitting calmly and arrogantly, ignoring the driver who was ready to kill him. The louder the guy yelled at him the more indifferent he seemed to be. He looked more like Jack Palance than ever. If it had been me I wouldn't have messed with this guy, even if he was a dog.

What a dog. Over the years that we worked together he has peed on my legs, eaten the leather dashboard out of my car, and stolen entire rump roasts off the kitchen table when no one was looking. Why did I put up with this crazy dog? I loved him and we were partners. We were in business together and taught each other as we went along. We had a contract.

I'd like to tell you how Silver came into my life. It began with my oldest and dearest friend, Alan Feinstein, a well-known actor who appeared on the soap opera "Love of Life" for several years and for many years after that on "The Edge of Night." He has also been in many movies and TV shows. We've been friends since we were kids in the fourth grade at PS 139 in Queens. We were also roommates in New York for two years and he was best man at my wedding. Although I don't have a better friend in the world, Silver put that relationship to its severest test.

Alan convinced me to move to Manhattan and share an apartment with him. We were in our early twenties and I knew it was time to leave home and go out on my own. So we loaded

Matt and his first dog, Smoky.

up my VW with suitcases full of clothes, souvenirs, and Alan's precious record collection of Elvis Presley and Beatles albums and crossed the 59th Street Bridge. It was an adventure. The first place we moved to was on West Fifty-eigth Street between Eighth and Ninth avenues. It was a furnished, one-bedroom apartment that was somewhat shabby as I think about it now. But at the time it seemed like an estate. Life was good. I had my friend, my job, my Volkswagen, and my apartment. All I needed was a dog.

I was scared being out on my own for the first time, living away from home. It was not as easy as I thought it would be. New York is overwhelming when you take it on for the first time and you're completely on your own. I knew that a dog was the one thing that would make me feel better in this intimidating new life. There had always been a dog in my life, ever since I was a kid. In addition to our family dog, my father was constantly bringing home strays that were lost or abandoned or somehow not wanted. Living with dogs was the most natural condition of my life. My first pet was a Dalmatian named Smoky, but the last one I had growing up was a Weimaraner named Miss Boo. She was an obedient and protective dog in addition to being a sweet, gentle friend that I loved very much. I've missed her since the day she died. I always promised myself I'd get another Weimaraner someday, once I was out in the world, on my own. Well, the day had come.

I was shy and insecure when I was a kid, but the dogs in our house made me feel good about myself even when I got into trouble, which was always. Being surrounded by dogs saved me and helped me use up the incredible energy that always got me into trouble. My love of dogs was a family dynamic that I couldn't live without.

I found a kennel with Weimaraners for sale in New Jersey from an ad in the newspaper and I dragged my unenthusiastic friend with me in the Volkswagen. I wanted him to be as excited about this as I was. When we got there we found six young Weimaraners for sale. Five of them were the most beautiful creatures in the world that came right up to you, licked your hand, and jumped with pleasure to see you. The sixth one was in the corner, all curled up and depressed looking. The young dog was thin and underweight. When I asked about him I was told that nobody wanted that one. His sad, droopy face stirred feelings in me I couldn't put into words, and I had to have him. I was determined to save that rejected animal no matter what. I paid for him, named him Silver, and put him in the backseat of the car. It was an exciting moment, and as I walked with him from the kennel to the Volkswagen, Silver became my dog.

On the drive back to New York we stopped at a Mc-Donald's for a half dozen Big Macs. I went in for the food and left Alan in the car with the puppy. It never occurred to me that the dog would frighten him. Although Silver was only six months old Alan was intimidated by his size. The poor guy didn't know how to behave around him. He was convinced that any move he made would get his arm torn off. He sat in the car in sheer terror. I had no idea he felt that way. When I got back I gave them each a couple of Big Macs and started the engine.

Minutes after the dog devoured the Big Macs he threw up all over the backseat. Talk about fast food. I cleaned up without complaint and tried not to look at Alan. After spreading out some papers on the front seat, I put the big puppy up front with us. We were like Moe, Larry, and Curly as the three of us sat together for the long drive home. Alan didn't know whether to pet him, touch him, or jump out of the car. He was six-foot-two, weighed two hundred pounds, and could bench press almost twice his own weight but was scared to death of this young dog. He never moved during the ride home. My good friend sat frozen in one position, just staring ahead, convinced that the slightest movement would make the dog attack him.

The first night with Silver was a delightful joy for me but a misery for Alan. The apartment had one bedroom with two single beds in it. After playing with the dog for a while I went to bed and fell into a deep, peaceful sleep. Alan struggled to get to sleep. He tossed and turned for hours before drifting off. He woke up in the middle of the night to go to the bathroom. The room was dark and as he turned his head on the pillow he discovered Silver sitting next to the bed, staring coldly at him. They were eyeball to eyeball. He jerked back and could barely control himself. He was convinced he was in mortal danger and let out something between a gasp and a squeal, but I never heard it. The man spent the next two hours in a cold sweat, staring up at the ceiling. He never moved. He was not dog owner material.

After the first week things got easier; Alan loosened up and began to adjust to the dog. I worked hard to show him how playful and affectionate dogs were, especially one that was as young as Silver. We played together for hours and I'd get him to roll on his back so I could rub his belly and scratch his long ears. By the second week Alan was feeling so good about the dog that he was putting his hand in Silver's mouth and bragging about it to me and all of his friends. He was very proud of himself and thought he was the dog master of the world. He was lulled into a good feeling about Silver . . . until the first of several disasters happened.

I was working as a salesman at the time for Yardley of London, and I kept all of my cosmetic samples in four large boxes in the living room closet. The first disaster was due to my lack of knowledge about dogs. I was too permissive some of the time and too harsh the rest of the time. I didn't know how to teach my dog to do the right thing even though I hollered at him when he did the wrong thing. It made him crazy. I didn't know you had to confine an untrained dog to one small place just to keep him out of mischief.

One morning I neglected to walk Silver before going to work, and his need to pee along with his fear of my hollering at him made him frantic. He was an energetic hunting dog living in a confined space and that contributed a lot to the problem. The poor dog became wildly frantic while we were away at work and in his mad dash around the apartment he got the closet door open.

Alan was the first one home that day and walked into pure destruction. He was stunned as he slowly moved from room to room. The apartment looked as if a tornado in Technicolor had hit it. The cardboard cartons containing the cosmetic samples were ripped into small pieces and sucked wet. There was pink powder all over the floor and furniture. Lipsticks were chewed up and ground into the carpet. Half-eaten mascara and rouge samples were smeared along the walls, the baseboards, the bedspreads—just about everywhere. Plastic bottles of aftershave lotion and cologne were punctured with teeth marks. They were ripped open and scattered everywhere, with their caps missing. There were small puddles of liquid fragrance on the floor, on the couch, and on both beds. The place looked as if it had been ransacked by a gang of cosmetic junkies in desperate need of a makeover. It was like walking through Elizabeth Arden's after an explosion. And there was a perfume stink that was never going to leave.

When I came home I found Alan sitting calmly in the middle of the debris. He was at the kitchen table drinking a glass of milk and reading the latest issue of *Variety*. He didn't look up from his paper and never said a word to me. There was nothing either one of us could say. It was eerie. Silver broke the silence as he trotted out of the bathroom, sat at my feet and looked up, waiting for my high-pitched, baby-voice hello and an affectionate belly rub. You had to see his face to believe it. The fur around his lips and the edges of his teeth were coated with bright red lipstick. His tongue was streaked with black and brown mascara. It must have tasted good. His coat was covered with powder and he smelled like a barbershop in the heat. I quietly walked him back to the bathroom and closed the door.

With no emotion at all, Alan rose from his chair, neatly folded his paper and said he was going out for dinner and would call me later to find out if the apartment was ready for his return. He never yelled or hollered. I thought he took it all rather well. I never heard his inner explosion. I spent more than three hours cleaning up but it was useless. There was no way for me to get rid of all the red and black smears or the smell of a massage parlor. We discreetly moved out the following week.

Considering what Silver had done to the place, the move was a good idea. Alan accepted the fact that Silver was now part of the family and that he couldn't get rid of him. We packed our things and traveled quickly and quietly. When you're twenty-one and you don't own the furniture, moving is easy. We found a new apartment on Fifty-seventh Street between Second and Third avenues. It was owned by a lovely lady from Japan who liked us even though she was hesitant about the dog. I'm sure she rented to us because she recognized Alan from "Love of Life."

The east end of Fifty-seventh Street was an exciting place for us to live. The buildings were beautiful and well kept and we were close to everything. The apartment was another one-bedroom flat but was spacious and elegantly furnished. We paid a hundred dollars a month more rent, but it was worth every penny. I'm sure the same apartment now rents for two or three thousand dollars a month. The building had a doorman and an elevator to take us all the way up to the second floor. We were on top of the world as far as I was concerned. We didn't know that the second Silver disaster was to come a few months later.

Alan and I were like the odd couple. He was neat and orderly and I was messy and disorganized. It never occurred to me to place a used dish or glass in the sink, and if I did, that's where it stayed. By now, Alan considered Silver as just another part of the mess. Our new apartment was beautifully furnished with the most interesting antiques, mostly from the Orient. Every end table had a hand-painted vase or lamp on it, and the couch and soft chairs were attractively framed in dark mahogany wood with a low-luster patina that made everything look expensive and tasteful. Nothing was ordinary or shabby. But the most striking furniture was in the bedroom. There were two large, imposing twin beds imported from China that dominated the room. They were made of dark, glossy cherrywood, polished with age. The headboards and footboards were made of thick slabs of wood with relief carvings of dragons projecting from the surface of the wood. The bedposts were extensions of the dragons' legs with a large, hand-carved claw at the top and bottom of each. There were eight claws in all and the detail work on each one was powerful looking.

We were in the East Fifty-seventh Street apartment for almost a year when the next Silver disaster occurred. Late one afternoon Alan came home from CBS as usual, hung up his jacket, and lay down on his bed to read the paper. Something didn't seem right but he couldn't put his finger on it. He sat up, looked around and then went back to his paper. Something was wrong. After a minute he shot up like a bolt and realized that he could see only one claw at the foot of the bed. He stood up and walked around to the front and placed his hand on the denuded bedpost. There was only raw wood where once a dragon's claw had grasped the post. He got on his knees and looked for it under the bed, all around the floor, in the kitchen, and throughout the apartment. It was gone. There were teeth marks and deep scratches on the bedpost and all that remained of the dragon's claw were splinters and wood dust on the carpet.

"Silver!" he shouted. The dog was in the bathroom and had no intention of coming out. Besides, he never responded to Alan's commands anyway. While Silver hid in the bathroom Alan threw himself onto the bed in a panic. By the time I got home from work he had this whole scenario worked out in his head where the landlady went berserk over her declawed Chinese bed and had us evicted and thrown in jail.

"All right," I said calmly. "Don't panic. I'll think of something. I know. We'll have the bed fixed."

Alan looked up and said, "You mean restored, right?"

"Okay, restored," I said with a sigh. Fixed meant a hundred dollars. Restored meant a thousand dollars. I looked around the apartment for Silver. I wanted to get my hands around his neck.

After one week and many phone calls I found a craftsman in the Yellow Pages who came to the apartment and looked at the bed. He whistled with admiration and told us how beautiful it was and what a shame that it had been defaced. He informed us that he could carve a new claw and have it mounted on the bedpost but that he had to take it to his shop for an unspecified period of time. I winced when he said it would cost one thousand dollars to do the work.

"What about me?" Alan complained. "What am I supposed to use for a bed?"

"What about me? I'm the one who has to dig up a thousand dollars," I answered. Once again I had to call my father to bail me out and lend me the money.

When they took the dragons and the claws away they left the mattress where the bed had been. I was very uneasy each night on my nice, comfortable bed looking down at Alan sleeping on the floor because my dog ate his claw. The bed was gone for two months. When it finally came back it looked exactly as it had before, but within one week Silver chewed another claw off and we had to start all over again. Alan threatened to leave but I was able to talk him out of it by letting him sleep in my bed while I took the mattress on the floor.

Chewing up a pillow or an occasional newspaper was merely annoying. But when Silver got into Alan's prized record collection it became the third and final dog disaster that we

Alan Feinstein, my oldest and dearest friend.

shared. He had been collecting Elvis Presley records since age eleven. Over the years Alan had also accumulated all of the Beatles and Sam Cooke albums ever made in addition to those of many other performers he enjoyed. One morning Silver took it into his head to zip through each album, leaving no disk or its cover unchewed. The entire collection of records was destroyed and there simply was no way to replace them. Alan was so upset that he soon afterward left us for Hollywood to explore new acting possibilities for several months. While Alan was on the West Coast I started dating Beverly almost every night and our relationship began to grow into something serious. We had become a couple. And Silver made three.

A month or two before Beverly and I were married in the summer of 1968 I asked her to come home from work during lunchtime one afternoon so that she could see the little dog that I was training. I knew she would enjoy meeting the silky ball of white fur. The miniature dog was a regal-looking Maltese, one of the toy breeds. The furry pellet of energy was a breed that we were not familiar with and I thought she would enjoy the brief encounter. Little did I know that the tiny dog would enthrall her. She fell in love with it instantly and mistakenly thought that I had brought it home as a gift for her. It was an awkward situation because I had to explain that I just wanted her to see the dog. Of course, the incident gave me food for thought. The only pets Beverly had had as a child were a goldfish and a parakeet named Petey. She adored the parakeet, who lived for eighteen years, which is something of a record for a bird living with a kid.

Soon after we were married, in July of that year, we moved out of the apartment we shared with Alan Feinstein and settled into our own place. In August, Beverly developed a bad case of the flu and was home in bed for several days. She felt miserable. I was working long hours then and didn't get home one night until eleven o'clock. I walked into the apartment with my briefcase and our dirty beach blanket all rolled up in my arms.

I said to her, "You know, this blanket has been lying in the car for two months and is so disgusting we ought to throw it in the washing machine." She thought it was insensitive of me to bring home laundry while she was sick. I tossed the dirty blanket on the bed and out popped a little, furry white head with a nose like a pebble of coal sitting over a little red mouth. The puppy's eyes were like large, dark marbles and looked around softly. It was Princess, the cutest, most adorable silky white Maltese you could possibly imagine. She couldn't have weighed more than two pounds at the time. I don't think I've ever had a more tender moment with my wife than I did at that moment. It was love at first sight. She squealed with delight as tears formed in the corners of her eyes, the kind that only a new puppy can create in someone who's never had a dog. From that moment on Princess was never far from her arms. She took her everywhere. The very next day she and her mother, who came in from New Jersey just to see the new addition to the family, took the dog for her first veterinary exam. In the cab Princess immediately threw up all over Beverly's expensive blue suede vest, which she prized more than anything else in her wardrobe. It was the finest garment she owned but she just didn't care that it was going to be permanently stained. Her mother sat in shock and couldn't believe that she simply cleaned it off without anger, disgust, or annoyance. Beverly was a very happy woman with her new "baby." She loved that little dog more than she knew at the time. And of course that began the saga of Silver's new life with a tiny but domineering dog.

Actually, Silver liked the new member of the family right away. His big problem, though, was that he was too big and too rambunctious to be allowed on the bed. Of course, Princess was always on the bed and she considered it her personal domain. All Silver had to do was approach the bed to say hello and the white mite would suddenly became a defender of territory and rush to the edge, take a protective stance, and bark her little heart out. If Silver persisted on approaching the soft blankets, still warm from our bodies, she would growl, grab his upper lip with her teeth, and not let go. On a number of

Beverly was a very happy woman with her new baby.

occasions she hung from his upper lip by her incisors as the big dog backed away. He would try to get as far away from the bed as possible with Princess dangling from his face by her teeth as he slowly backed out of the room. Beverly has always said, "I don't know how or why he tolerated all that from such a tiny dog, but he did. To Princess, Silver was just a big dodo and she ruled the roost." I guess everyone, including Silver, had to love the little Maltese or else.

Of course, Silver got his licks in, too. Every day Beverly would go to a great deal of trouble preparing the little sovereign's breakfast, and the instant she put the dish on the floor Silver would sneak up on it and slurp it into his mouth in one gulp. "You'd think I'd have learned the routine," she used to say. "Sometimes, the poor dog missed her meal and I didn't even know it." Beverly was always saying to Silver, "Don't you hurt her. I'll kill you. I'll kill you!" Of course, I don't believe Silver would ever have harmed the little dog. He never did. What a pair! They were our family at the time until our son Jesse was born.

chapter four

tails from the crypt

Poofie, Poochie, and Muff-Muff were sweethearts that gave it up easily. In my first six months as a professional I had successfully trained about twenty dogs that were all cute balls of curly fur with little pink tongues hanging out the sides of their mouths. They were cream puffs and made me think I was the dog meister of New York City. I thought I could handle anything that wagged a tail. My education was about to begin.

On a warm summer day in July 1968, I parked my car in front of a five-story brownstone on West Seventy-eighth Street to see a new client. The street was quiet as a few young trees sprouting out of the cement swayed gently in the breeze, making this part of Manhattan pleasant and deceptively inviting. I was there to see a woman whose "pet," a three-year-old Alaskan Malamute, would not tolerate anyone coming into her apartment. My initial response on the phone was that any dog could be trained. I very glibly told her that I could easily train her dog and solve his problem in six weeks. She sounded skeptical and asked me to come to her home and see him. I agreed and there I was.

The woman lived in the basement apartment of a typical New York City brownstone. I went down three short steps along the outside of the building and walked through a wrought-iron gate to get to her private doorway under the front stoop. Her apartment had two windows facing the street which shut the world out with closed Venetian blinds. When I knocked on her door a sudden, overpowering sound of frenzied growls, snorts, and barks from behind the windows pierced the quiet of the street. I jumped. It was the loud, frightening roar of an animal that wanted to kill something and eat it.

"*Grrraaagh, grrraaagh, grrraaagh!*" It was an unforgettable sound. Then, something beastly took a frantic run at the window and hit the Venetian blinds with fury, snapping them back

I thought I could handle any dog that wagged a tail.
My education was about to begin.

and forth with a clattering noise of twisting metal smacking against the glass. All I could see were large, muscular paws trying to claw through the blinds. A muffled human voice from behind the window shouted and the horrible growling stopped. As I stood at the door waiting, I felt a sickening twinge in the pit of my stomach. Only my pride, and my need to succeed, prevented me from running back to my car, rolling up the windows, and driving the hell out of there. I stood my ground at the door but I could tell this was not a doggie.

"Who is it?" asked a tense voice from behind the door.

"It's Matthew. The dog trainer. Would you put the dog in another room, please?"

"Okay, I'll put Fang away. Give me a couple of minutes."

"Fang," I said to myself. "Oh, my God."

Then I heard, "Get in there" and *"Grrraaagh, grrraaagh"* accompanied with the sound of a struggle to close a door.

I could hear the front door being unlocked and then un-chained. The knob turned and as the door opened I tightened the grip on my briefcase and was ready to use it to cover my face if the creature lunged at me. To my surprise and great relief, the dog was gone and I was greeted by a very tense woman with an uneasy look on her face. She was around thirty-five years old, five-foot-five, 115 pounds, and very thin. She wore slacks, a short-sleeve blouse, and a pair of thick leather gloves. I remember thinking, "Why is she wearing gloves in the summer?"

"Hello. We spoke on the phone yesterday."

"Come in," she said in a soft but forced voice. She led me inside a neat, clean apartment that was surprisingly pleasant, considering she was living in the basement with a dog named Fang. It was nicely furnished and much larger than it appeared from the outside. We walked through a small, dark hallway, past a closed door and into a spacious living room. As we sat down on two upholstered chairs facing each other, I noticed deep-set wrinkles on her forehead. I removed a pad from my briefcase, ready to take notes. It was a process I was developing.

"Okay, tell me about your dog."

She spoke to me quietly, in a somber tone of voice, as if she was confessing to a priest.

"I got Fang when he was a puppy. He was an adorable baby dog and I loved him right away. He used to curl up around my feet at night and sleep on the bed with me. Of course, that's out of the question now but he *was* the cutest thing. To tell the truth, he growled at everything from the first day I got him. If you took a chew toy out of his mouth, he growled. If you went near his food bowl, he growled. If you tried to put the leash on him, he growled. It seemed so cute at the time. I never imagined what that growl would be like once he matured.

"I purposely chose a large breed because I live alone and I wanted protection. But what I have now is a very aggressive dog that runs my life. I can't make him do anything unless I force him and I'm the only one he'll tolerate in the apartment. He doesn't allow anyone in without scaring them to death. None of my friends or relatives will come to see me anymore because they don't want to be around him. I have no social life and a man hasn't asked me out in six months. Also, I have a very hard time walking Fang on the street. He pulls my arm out and threatens anyone who comes near him."

I was silent for a few seconds as I tried to absorb what she was telling me. I asked if she ever possibly considered another home for this dog (maybe someplace in Borneo, I thought to myself).

She shook her head and quietly answered, "No, that's out of the question. He's my responsibility. And believe it or not, I still love him. I could never get rid of him. Can you help me?"

It came as no surprise to me. Most people love their dogs and could no sooner throw them away than they could throw away another person. I understood that. The first thing I told her is how I work; that I come to the home and obedience train the dog with the owner. I then explained that if the dog was obedience trained the owner would at least have control over him. He was never going to be Benji but at least he would obey her commands.

"What about people coming into the apartment?" she asked.

I nodded my head and said, "Once he's trained you can put him in the corner in a Down-Stay. He'll probably stare hard at your guests and make them uneasy, but he won't attack them if you don't let him. That's probably the best you can hope for."

She thought that was a lot better than her current situation and agreed to have him trained.

"Good," I said. "Now, let's see the dog. Bring him out, and please, keep him on a leash."

"Okay," she said enthusiastically as she got up and reached for the largest, thickest metal choke collar I had ever seen. It was hooked to a thick leather leash sitting on the end table. She stepped out into the hallway and went into the room where the dog was eagerly waiting behind the door. I heard a loud, *"Grrraaagh"* and then the door closed. Muffled from behind the door I heard her shout as she tried to get the leash and collar on, "Easy, Fang, easy! Get down. Get down. For chrissake, stop it!"

"*Grrraaagh, grrraaagh*" hammered through the walls from the other room.

I could tell that Fang knew his dinner was in the living room. He could smell a Jewish deli in there just waiting for him. I thought to myself, "Why wasn't I a plumber or something wonderful like that? Why did I want to be a dog trainer, anyway?" All of a sudden the door opened and something that resembled a bear head came out—just a head. I swear, I never saw a bigger dog head in my life and it was all mouth and teeth, dripping with saliva. It could have been the shark from *Jaws.* The rest of the dog's body seemed to take an eternity to come through the doorway. "Oh, my God," I thought, "this is a big dog." He took one look in the room and went for me in a hard, pulling lunge. He really wanted me.

"*Grrraaagh, grrraaagh, grrraaagh, grrraaagh!*" Translation: Brunch! His upper lip was curled all the way and every tooth in his mouth was grinding and slathering as he strained on the leash. The woman had to pull hard on it to keep him on his side of the room as she shouted, "No, Fang, no!"

Every time she pulled on the leash the dog thundered from the back of his throat, "*Grrraaagh, grrraaagh!*" My mouth dried out and my eyes opened wider than they ever had. It was a Wolf Man movie and I was about to become chuck steak. The dog scared the hell out of me. With each snorting growl he snapped at whichever hand of hers he could get his mouth onto. Suddenly I realized why she wore the leather gloves. I wondered if she had any skin left underneath.

The animal was easily 125 pounds of fury. I couldn't get

myself to move off the couch. I became the fourth cushion. I tried to get smaller and smaller but I couldn't disappear fast enough.

I vaguely remember thinking, "I'm not touching this sucker, I don't care what anyone thinks." It was humiliating considering that I was a dog trainer. Finally, I pulled myself together and managed to blurt out with a phony little smile, "Well, it looks like he doesn't like strangers."

She nodded in agreement as she struggled to keep the dog off me and said, "What can you do about it?"

"Not very much," I said with controlled hysteria, as I tried to keep my hands from shaking. The dog finally stopped pulling on the leash, sat down and locked his eyes onto mine with pure menace. He curled his upper lip again and let out a low, deep-throated growl as he stared at me. It was like sitting in the room with Dracula. My heart was trying to pound its way out of my chest. My very existence seemed to offend this dog.

The poor woman was at a loss. She looked at me needfully and said, "You see. This is what he does. I don't know what to do about it."

I had to see the dog's response to a leash correction but I couldn't make myself get off the couch. I said to her, "Jerk him to the right. Let's see what happens."

"What do you mean?" she asked.

I stood up and reached for the leash with my arm.

A fast and violent sequence of *"Grrraaagh, grrraaagh, grrraaagh, grrraaagh"* is all I remember from the moment. The blood flushed instantly to my feet and my face turned white as I pulled my hand away at the speed of light and sat down again. I might have climbed up the back of the couch but I don't know for sure.

Like a warden talking to a condemned prisoner I said to her, "Relax. Just jerk the leash to the right and say no in a firm tone of voice."

Holding the leash with both hands the woman jerked it hard to the right and bellowed out, "No!"

"*Grrraaagh, grrraaagh, grrraaagh*" was the dog's response as he turned his head and chewed on her hands.

"Are you all right?" I asked (from the couch).

"Oh, yeah. That's why I wear the gloves. I'm used to this. Look, I don't know what you want. Why don't you show me? It's your turn to do something, Mr. Margolis." She tried to hand me the leash but I didn't reach for it.

"You may have jerked him too hard," I said with that phony little smile on my face.

The woman was so thin and the dog's head was so large that he completely blocked her body from view. All I could see were her arms hanging on to the frail line that prevented me from becoming meat loaf. I told her that she had to release the tension on the leash immediately after jerking it. I got up to show her what to do but the dog leaped toward me, letting out his terrifying "*Grrraaagh*" sound.

"Listen," I said. "This isn't going to work. I can't handle Fang. He may be nipping at your hands but he wants to swallow me whole. There's no way I can do this. Let's try a different approach. How about if I show you what to do and *you* train the dog?" Out of pure desperation she agreed and we made an appointment for a training session.

The following week I parked my car in front of her building and walked to her door. When I rang the doorbell I experienced the same nasty routine. Fang barked and growled and attacked the windows.

I yelled into the apartment, "Don't open the door. I'll meet you outside with the dog."

"Okay, we'll be out in a minute."

I wasn't about to enter her apartment again until that blood-sucking savage was under control. While waiting I tried to figure out where to position myself so that I could demonstrate what she had to do and remain chewproof. I stepped off the sidewalk, into the street about twelve inches from the curb, and waited. In a few minutes the door opened and that enormous bear head appeared, pulling the rest of its huge body out with it like a bull entering the ring. Following behind was a six-foot length of leash held by a stretched-out arm attached to the thin body of the owner. The dog pulled her up the three steps and out onto the sidewalk. He was a hungry lion. He looked up and down the block. The minute he saw me his eyes darkened with hate and he let out a horrible growling bark. It wasn't so much that he was barking at me because it was me, but because someone had entered his territory. Of course, unlike most dogs, he considered Manhattan, the other four boroughs, and maybe all of New York State to be his territory. Whenever she walked down the street with him people and dogs would have to get out of the way because Fang was coming.

His nasty reaction to me made me keep backing away from them until I reached the other side of the street. I yelled over to her, "Stay where you are. I'll instruct you from here."

The woman shook her head and yelled back, "I can't hear you and I can't see you."

As much as I didn't want to do it I moved closer to her and Fang, step by step. I found myself crouching behind my parked car but I wasn't able to show her anything from there.

woof!

There was no way that I could come out and get near her. Finally, the solution occurred to me. I climbed onto the roof of my car and was able to get close enough to them without getting bitten. It was like being on a stage. The dog looked up at me and seemed to be as astonished as the people walking by. In a few minutes he calmed down and concentrated on his owner.

I removed a newspaper from my briefcase, rolled it into a funnel, and put it to my lips. It made an excellent megaphone.

"Can you hear me?" I shouted to her. My voice rang out with an amplified echo.

She nodded.

The noise from the passing traffic forced me to shout and the makeshift megaphone created an echo. As I stood on top of my car I acted out everything I taught her. "Okay. Here's the proper way to hold the leash."

I spoke in a slow, deliberate tone of voice. "Good. Place the dog on your left. Very good. Start walking. That's right. Make a right turn. You're doing very well." My instructions echoed up and down Seventy-eighth Street as my client and her dog began to learn something about dog obedience training. The scene was bizarre. There I was standing on the roof of my car in the middle of New York City yelling through a rolled-up newspaper to a woman and a dog that was nuts. I hollered out instructions to her and her four-legged pupil for one hour and continued to do so for each weekly training session. They both turned out to be good students. By the end of ten weeks the dog would Heel, Sit, Stay, Come, and Lie Down . . . for her. I charged her three hundred dollars and never once touched the dog. When it was over, she tried to say thank you to me but by then I was parking my car farther and farther up the block. Fang was not as grateful as his owner. "You're welcome!" I yelled back at her, from the roof of my car.

From the start, I called my service the National Institute of Dog Training, even when I worked out of my kitchen. I used to enjoy answering the phone as if I were sitting in the executive office of my own kennel establishment, much like the one I now have in Los Angeles. Back in the early seventies, dog training as an essential part of pet ownership was an idea whose time had come. As my advertising and promotion grew, so did my reputation, so people were becoming aware of me. Young dog trainers came to me for jobs and I hired several of them in order to keep up with the demand for the service. I was no longer standing alone on the roof of my car, bellowing out training commands to a dangerous dog.

By 1971 I had trained many extremely aggressive dogs and had learned a great deal from my experiences. My ad in the Yellow Pages reflected this and, to my amazement, attracted many clients with problem dogs. Even though most dogs are sweet, friendly companions and only need simple obedience training, there are far too many that are aggressive and dangerous. Over the years I have trained my share of them and have come to the conclusion that you are not a professional trainer if you can't handle such dogs. But I learned the hard way that there was always a dog out there waiting to challenge your skill and experience. You never know what you're getting into when the phone rings.

One morning in 1971 I received a call from a man in New Jersey. He had such a thick Spanish accent that I could barely understand him. He somehow managed to communicate to me that he owned a German Shepherd that he kept in the backyard of his home and had some kind of a problem with it. I agreed to drive out to see him and his dog that afternoon and find out what was wrong. It took twenty-five minutes to get to Jersey City and forty-five minutes to find the man's house based on his instructions.

Although the neighborhood was a little run-down, with an occasional auto tire and trash can here and there, it was lush with trees, shrubbery, thick grass, and crushed-pebble roads. Squirrels hopped in and out of the bushes and you could actually hear the birds in the trees. I pulled into the driveway of an old house with peeling green paint, a sagging porch, and a small garage attached to the side and slightly to the rear. Both structures sat at the bottom of a small hill. The yard in the back was part of the hill with a high wooden fence around it. It was partially hidden from view by the house, the garage, and some old trees with thick, gnarled trunks.

The door opened before I had a chance to knock. I was greeted by a man around forty years old, obviously Hispanic, obviously nervous. So many of the owners of problem dogs have that worried look on their faces. You almost know what is wrong by their facial expressions. A phony smile frequently indicates that they hit the dog and are ashamed to admit it. An angry expression often means that the dog has chewed their possessions or dumped on the carpet. If they express ease and nonchalance it is sometimes a coverup for a dog that has bitten someone. If they are very nervous and upset, the dog is driving them crazy. The man in front of me was half out of his mind. He obviously had a big dog problem.

He invited me inside the house, where there were at least six other men and women of various ages sitting in the living room hanging on our every word as they munched on some kind of nuts or chips out of brown paper bags. There was a strange, unpleasant odor hanging in the air. It smelled like mildew and cooked fat mixed together.

The only one there who spoke any English at all was the man who answered the door. He was obviously the head of the house. We communicated to each other with broken English, hand signals, sign language, and a few Spanish words filling in the gaps. He managed to make me understand that nobody had been able to get in the backyard for the past three years. I asked him what he meant and he half spoke and half acted out that repairmen, power company people, telephone workers—nobody—could get in the backyard because of the dog. Evidently, no one in the family, including himself, was able to get out there, either. The dog attacked anyone who set one foot in the yard.

They had gotten him as a puppy and kept him outside all of his life because they wanted a guard dog. As he got bigger he became a lot more aggressive than they counted on and eventually had gotten totally out of their control. He had become so ferocious that they couldn't bring him inside the house if they wanted. The only time they saw him was when they fed him. They wanted me to train their dog so that they could bring him inside and maybe, just maybe, get in their own yard again.

I asked the man how he fed the dog if he didn't let anyone in the yard. His face lit up with pride as he raised his finger in the air and nodded his head with a smile. He said something in Spanish to one of the women and she hurried out of the room. He then pointed to a hunk of wood on the wall and invited me to inspect it. All I could see was a rectangular-shaped piece of plywood hanging on the wall like a blank picture frame. I shrugged my shoulders. I didn't get it. The man then grabbed a small wooden knob at the bottom and pulled the solid piece of wood slightly away from the wall. It was a trapdoor!

Hanging from hinges at the top, it was a secret hatch hung over the sofa like a clumsy repair job. The man pulled it up and hooked it open to a catch in the ceiling. Deep in the opening, about fourteen inches from the inside wall, was a small window looking out at the yard. It looked like the opening of a bunker. All it needed was a cannon sticking out of it. The only thing I could see out the window was a small patch of grass because of the severe slope of the ground. The head of the house made it clear to me that he had built this himself. I was amused and impressed. Mostly amused. The woman returned from the kitchen with a metal bowl filled with dog food and gave it to the man.

He then stepped onto the sofa and held out his right arm as he looked through the hatchway and out the little window. A younger man efficiently placed a short pole with a bent nail at the end of it into his extended hand. The woman standing next to him slapped the bowl of dog food into his other hand. It was like watching a team of surgeons in an operating room. Everyone there gathered around the trapdoor in silent antic-ipation as he balanced himself on the sofa holding the bowl and the pole. In one smooth gesture the man slid the pole into the hole in the wall and quietly pushed the window open with it as he carefully shoved the bowl out the window with his arm, which he quickly pulled back. He then shouted, "Hey, Macho! Comida, Macho!"

As he got the window half closed with the bent nail of the

pole, you could hear a frantic gallop as bony paws pounded the hard ground. Suddenly, four hairy legs as thick as baseball bats appeared, making loud, snarling growls and grunts. The dog's furious head bent down between the front legs and buried itself into the bowl as it bit into the metal with an open mouth. All I could see were flashing teeth, a fast-moving tongue, and chunks of food sliding into his mouth as they disappeared in four chomps, a slurp, and a gulp. An occasional angry eye darted frightening glances inside the house. It was like witnessing a sacrifice to King Kong with the tribe watching, hoping he would be satisfied for a while and leave them alone. I never saw anything like it in my life. It was feeding time on Kong Island. The only thing missing was the drums.

I thought to myself, "Oh, no. I can't do this. They're throwing food through the trapdoor and nobody goes out there. I'm just getting over Fang. I'm not going to be Daniel in the lion's den. How do I get out of this?"

There was no way that I was going to train that dog. I didn't want the flesh torn off my bones. I needed a way to get myself out of this job gracefully. At that time I was charging two and three hundred dollars to train a dog. I figured I'd scare them off.

"Twelve hundred dollars for six lessons," I said in a hard tone of voice.

They grouped together in a huddle speaking furiously in Spanish to each other as one or two of them threw an occasional glance at me. Finally, they stopped chattering and fell silent. The man who spoke English asked me to stay where I was as they left the room. I couldn't wait to get out of there but I didn't want to insult them. I stood in the middle of the room for a couple of minutes, waiting for them to return so I could say good-bye. There wasn't a sound in the house until Macho suddenly started a frenzied barking and growling through the trapdoor. I looked into the hatchway and could see his teeth chewing on the window frame. He wanted dessert and thought I was it. It occurred to me that the dog just didn't want me there.

The six people walked back into the room like a diplomatic delegation and stood there in a stiff, formal manner. The head man stepped forward and said, "Here. When will you start?" He handed me a crumpled paper bag. I looked inside and was astonished to find twelve hundred dollars in cash. All I remember thinking was, "Oh, no, no, no. Why me?"

With dread in my heart I returned the following week with one of the young trainers I had recently hired. There was no way I could deal with this dog by myself. He was a huge, dominant-aggressive German Shepherd, extremely territorial, and totally unsocialized with people. He was worse than any junkyard dog I had ever seen. This was a wild, dangerous animal.

We started out like a pair of rodeo clowns by climbing on adjacent roofs. I was on top of the garage and the other trainer got on top of the house. We had to get close enough to the dog to get him under control without being eaten alive. The only way I could accomplish that was to lasso the dog and hold him in place while I tried to get him to accept us. Our presence drove the dog nuts. He kept jumping up higher and higher. He wanted us badly. He got pretty close a couple of times, too. So here were two guys from Manhattan with lariats made of clothesline trying to rope a dog named Macho for half an hour. The roofs were about twelve feet high but the dog could jump almost eight feet off the ground. It was tricky.

We finally got one of the lassos around him. My assistant held the line tightly as I jumped into the yard and quickly threw the other line around him.

As we held Macho in place with two clotheslines, I came as close as I dared and talked soothingly to him. He snarled. He growled. He did his best to bite me. When he lunged at me the other trainer would jerk his line. When he lunged at the other trainer I jerked my line. It was like breaking a wild horse. Eventually, we got a muzzle on him and were then able to get a training collar and a leash around his neck without getting bitten. The dog kept coming at us and coming at us like you can't imagine. I didn't think he would ever run out of steam. If you want to know the truth, I never held it against him. His behavior was quite understandable. He had not been this close to anyone since he was a puppy. I felt sorry for him. It's not how a good dog should live. He deserved a better life. It took us about two hours to get him calmed down so that we could begin to work with him.

Once we accomplished that the people of the house poured into the yard in a party mood. I guess they had been watching us from a distance. They were very happy. One of the younger men had a guitar and began to play something up-tempo and festive. They put glasses of wine in our hands and made a fiesta out of the occasion. Evidently they felt that we had liberated their yard. We were the Magnificent Seven, minus five. The head of the house was happy. He even danced a bit with a couple of the women as he made his way over to us. He shook my hand, congratulated us, and without missing a beat said that since we had Macho on a leash we might as well get him to a vet for a rabies shot.

Maybe it was the wine or maybe it was their very flattering

happiness with our work. I don't know. The word *yes* came off my tongue so easily before I had a chance to think about it. Besides, I did take all that money from him. I started having second thoughts about this as we put the dog in the man's pickup truck. By the time we piled in ourselves I was sure this was a mistake, but it was too late.

We drove on some bumpy roads for ten minutes. When we got to the vet's office we knocked on the door and waited. I had a headache by then. It was either the wine, the dog, or the music. It was probably all three. The doctor opened the door and I told him that we had a dog that needed some shots. He said, "Come on in," with an innocent, unsuspecting manner. I never mentioned what the dog was like. Macho entered the man's clinic like a tied-up Brahman bull frantic to be released in the ring. His paws slipped and scratched the floor with panicky hysteria and the minute I brought him inside he turned beast and made a horrible lunge for the veterinarian, giving him the full snarling treatment. Kong was angry. The poor man was terrified and turned white as a ghost. He was backed against his own glass medicine case trying to dig a new door out of the wall. Little glass bottles spilled over as the metal cabinet tilted against the wall with a bang.

"I'm not touching this dog. Get him out," he said in a trembling voice.

I pleaded with him and pointed out how hard it was to get him there and that he never had any shots in his entire life. The vet softened just a bit and said he was willing to supervise me if I wanted to inject the dog myself and that was as far as he would go. I thought about that for a minute. God, I had never given a dog a shot before, but what could I do? I nodded and wished I would wake up from this bad dream.

With shaking hands the doctor filled the syringe with vaccine and handed it to me. I took it from him and meekly asked him to hold the leash. He got hysterical and hollered at me, "Are you crazy? Look, let's just get this over with and then get the hell out of here before I change my mind." There were tears of fear in my eyes. I just couldn't imagine the dog's reaction to me when I jabbed him with the needle. The vet told me where to stick him and how to do it. I followed his instructions perfectly and pushed the vaccine into the dog's massive body. Thank god Macho hated the doctor as much as he did because he never took his eyes off him. He was so concentrated on the vet that he hardly noticed the injection. I quickly threw a crumpled twenty dollar bill on the examining table and rushed the dog and the other two men out of there.

It had been quite a day. I had added to my list of accomplishments lassoing a dog and vaccinating him. I felt like a Jewish cowboy, sort of. When I finally made it home and into my bed, I slept well.

It took three weeks to get the dog to accept me as a dominant figure and four months in all to get him obedience trained. To his surprise I often reached in my pocket and dropped nibbles of cooked liver in front of him. He would gobble them up and look for more as he stared hard at me. I talked to him calmly. I talked to him firmly. I almost made love to him. In time I was able to pet the dog and have a nice relationship with him. Macho made it. In four months he became a house dog with a future. I was very proud of my work with him and I remember him fondly. Still, I'll never forget seeing him for the first time through the trapdoor. My legs still buckle a bit at the thought; I have no desire ever to return to Kong Island at feeding time.

chapter five

to train or not to train

Back then, when I walked down the streets of Manhattan with Silver at my side, I was vigorous and bursting with energy. When I went to work selling aftershave and tampons, I wasn't. My dog was my pal and I took him everywhere, even on dates. Like every dog I ever lived with, he made me feel important and special. It was an odd thing, but the closer I got to the dog, the more distant I became to my job. Selling toiletries and cosmetics to drugstores was worse than boring; it was disheartening. I was a leaky bucket losing my energy, my ambition, and my head. I had become upwardly mobile on the StairMaster to nowhere.

For all of 1967 I tried not to care that my friend and roommate, Alan, had become something of a star and was recognized by soap opera fans and headwaiters wherever we went. He seemed to have more fun, more money, more clothes, more everything than I did. His life was very glamorous from where I was sitting, which was on the sidelines. Call it envy or jealousy, but I wanted to be a star, too, and be on television, get fan mail, and meet all the interesting people he met. Alan made it seem easy. So, like many foolish kids, I thought becoming a star was a breeze, easily accomplished with a will and a whim.

"You know what," I said to Silver as he cocked his head to one side and licked my face, "I can do that. What's the big deal. I'll be an actor, too."

What I hadn't considered at the time was that Alan was totally dedicated to his craft and worked hard to get where he was. It had *always* been his ambition to be a professional actor. He had been in all the school plays throughout junior high and high school. After two years of college he took the plunge in New York and enrolled in the Dramatic Workshop. Every day he *made rounds*, which means he walked his feet off, making daily visits to the offices of talent agents, producers, and casting agents, knocking on doors, dropping off pictures and résumés, and lumping his share of daily rejection. It is a discouraging, humbling process that leaves most people disappointed and some completely heartbroken. Only the strong and determined survive the acting game and just a few lucky ones actually get somewhere. Sometimes talent is a factor and sometimes it's not. I never considered any of that. Only years later did I understand how much Alan must have resented my casual decision.

"You know," I said, "this could lead to you and me doing a show together or maybe even a series." Funny, I never noticed that he was grinding his teeth as I said it.

He had dedicated his life to acting and there I was, jumping in on an impulse. I had invaded my friend's territory without taking any of the risks or doing the hard work involved. It was like saying I think I'll do a little brain surgery on the weekends. Without thinking too much about it, I assumed he would be happy for me. He wasn't. But Alan never once complained. He generously took me under his wing and instructed me about the need for professional photos and résumés, and about getting an answering service to take all the phone messages for acting jobs that I expected. He taught me how to make rounds and to read the trade journals. On his insistence I enrolled in an acting class and tried to learn something about the skills and techniques of the actor's craft. After two improvisational exercises I was thrown out of the classroom for getting carried away with a young lady. They couldn't figure out if I was overacting or not acting at all. It was no thrill going back to school, anyway.

Ironically, I had a "look" that was right for some of the TV commercials being made at the time. Agents and casting people told me I resembled a blend of (the young) Marlon Brando and (the young) Burt Reynolds. My acting teacher thought I resembled a blend of (the young) Bud Abbott and (the old) Sabu. To go along with my "look," I changed my name to the more Hollywood-sounding Matthew Neal. Today, when I think of names like Art Garfunkel, John Malkovich, and Whoopi Goldberg I smile at the thought of *Matthew Neal.*

The photographs I had taken emphasized the "look" and did their job effectively. I received a call one week after dropping off pictures and résumés at agents' offices. It was from Mort Schwartz of Schwartz-Luskin, Inc., Artists' Representatives. He thought I was a good type and offered to represent me. I was in heaven. Getting in that agency was a great score for a beginner like me and it was a real ego booster. They printed my photo on a page with twenty-five other one-inch photos. So there I was sandwiched among the faces of twenty-five unknown actors on something they called a head sheet. The only memorable name on the head sheet was Jake La-Motta, the boxer. Obviously, this was long before his film biography, *Raging Bull.* Schwartz thought I had something and

An agent told me I had a "look" for show business.

started sending me out to auditions right away. I'll never forget the afternoon I ran home and reported to Alan in near hysteria that I had gotten cast in the first TV commercial that I tried out for.

All he could say was, "I got the first commercial I read for, too. But I never got another one."

I was so excited I could hardly breathe. Beverly was almost speechless. God, she was so supportive and encouraging. She couldn't get over it and was genuinely happy for me. Our relationship began to get serious after that. Things couldn't have been better. When I went to shoot the commercial the following week I discovered that Ed McMahon was the principal performer in what turned out to be a sixty-second spot for Utica

The look.

They only used my arms and legs.
The rest, they said, was Joe Namath.

Club Beer. I was one of several disco dancers in the back-ground, but if you looked carefully (and quickly) you could recognize me. I think the script referred to me as "an atmo-spheric element."

While I was on the Schwartz-Luskin head sheet I was cast in at least four commercials. The best of them was for Eastern Airlines, in which I was one of a bunch of soldiers sitting in a plane. That's about all there was of my brief acting career on television. I was also cast for a "print job," which involved posing for a still photograph for the cover of *Sports Illustrated.* They put me in an NFL football uniform and shot a lot of color pictures of me in front of a white backdrop. I still have one of the photographs as a souvenir. To my disappointment and complete amazement, they told me they only used my arms and legs. The rest, they said, was Joe Namath. Don't ask. I cannot explain it and I never saw the cover.

During this brief flurry of actor mania I thought I was riding high. Little did I know I was heading for a major tumble. Although I was being sent out for commercials by the Schwartz-Luskin agency, I knew I needed to get cast in something more substantial if I was going to be taken seriously and break into big-time television or movies. I kept making rounds and submitting my picture and résumé to other agents who might want to send me out for real acting parts. It paid off quickly.

At ten-thirty one morning I dropped off a picture and résumé at the office of Hesseltine, Bookman and Seff. At that time Stark Hesseltine was the hottest actors' agent in New York. He was a talent representative with considerable influence and prestige. I remember calling my answering service at eleven-thirty the same morning and being informed that Mr. Hesseltine wanted me to call him. It was urgent. With trembling hands I returned the call and spoke to his secretary, who said he wanted to see me right away, that he had something for me. It was just about the most important call that a young actor could get. I flew to his office on Fifty-seventh Street as if my feet had wings. My chest thumped with anticipation and I was delirious from the possibilities it represented. Everything I wanted was wrapped up in this most precious of interviews and it was all happening only three months after my decision to become an actor.

I kept repeating to myself, "This is it! This is it!"

When I got to the office I was immediately ushered past the reception area where several actors were sitting. I was led to the inner sanctum as if I were already a star. Hesseltine's private office was tastefully opulent with wood paneling, framed paintings, and a big, shiny red telephone. The view from the window revealed an impressive slice of Manhattan. And there he was, seated in a large, executive swivel chair. It was Hesseltine himself. "What were his parents thinking of when they named him Stark?" I wondered.

The room was covered with thick carpet and bathed in subdued light. Everything was quiet in his office and my voice instantly lowered to a hush. As I approached his big desk I was surprised to discover how youthful and preppy this important agent looked. He had blond hair and a bland but nice face sitting on a tall, slender frame. He wore an expensive, olive-colored suit with a striped tie. Although his manner was pleasant, almost sensitive, he was a serious man who understood his position in the acting business and I wasn't sure whether to shake his hand or bow at the waist. I guess anyone sitting behind an expensive wooden desk with an antique brass lamp would seem imposing, but there was something about him that intimidated me. After all, it was in his power to change my life.

He silently read my résumé as I just stood there, waiting to be acknowledged. Everything on it was phony. Before I wrote it I was told by other actors that all résumés were exaggerated. So, I credited myself with parts in plays written by playwrights I'd never even heard of. I listed appearances in plays by William Shakespeare, George Bernard Shaw, Arthur Miller, Tennessee Williams, Henrik Ibsen, Bertold Brecht, and several others. Considering that I had no acting experience whatsoever I guess I went a bit far.

Finally, he looked up and said, "God, you've worked a lot."

"I love my craft," I answered glibly, trying to cover up my uneasiness.

"Sit down, Matt. Would you like some coffee?"

"No thanks," I answered.

He whistled and tapped the résumé with his finger. "When did you do all this?"

My chair turned to quicksand as I struggled to answer. "Uh, from nineteen sixty-three to, uh, nineteen, uh, the present time."

"Where did you play Stanley Kowalski?"

"Who?"

"Stanley, from *Streetcar*," he said with a wry smile. "You must have done it in stock."

"Stock?"

"In summer stock?" he asked.

"Oh, stock! Sure. Summer stock. Winter stock." ("Chicken stock," I thought. "Who the hell is Stanley Kowalski?")

He nodded his head and said, "Good. Very good. Here's the deal. We've been asked to submit someone for an important part in a movie with Gregory Peck. The producer wants a new face with a New York quality. If you're the one you'll have to fly to the Coast to test for it. Okay?"

My energy surged as I responded, "No problem."

Thoughts were racing in my brain a mile a minute. "This is it. I'm being discovered. Alan may have a hard time with this, but I'm sure he'll be happy for me. I can't wait to go home and tell him."

"Matt? Matt?"

I looked up and tried to focus on Hesseltine.

"I'd like you to do a soliloquy or a monologue for me from one of the plays you were in," he said. "I need to get a sense of how you work. It's just a formality. With your background it should be a piece of cake. Pick anything off your

85

résumé. Do something from Shakespeare. How about Hotspur from *Henry IV*? Was he in Part One or Part Two?''

"I don't know. I flunked history."

Hesseltine laughed and said, "That's cute. Okay. Let's do it."

Without hesitating I said, "No problem. I'll be back in twenty-four hours. I need time to prepare."

"There *is* no time," he said, shaking his head. "You have to do it now. The plane tickets are for tomorrow morning. It's a key role and the producers want to know if you can act. I told them I don't know. I only know that you look right for the part."

For the first time I was forced to deal with the fact that I knew nothing about acting. I had never studied a part. I had never even read a play. My concept of an important theater experience was a double feature on Forty-second Street. I didn't know the difference between selling a character and selling a box of tampons. To me it was all the same thing. All I could think of was a soliloquy from *Hamlet* that we had had to learn to pass English in my senior year of high school.

"Okay, okay. Here goes."

I stepped back from the desk, placed one hand on my chest and the other in the air as if I were reaching for a tossed ball. My brow squeezed into an accordion as I sucked in a deep breath and did what I always did in situations like this. I jumped in, feetfirst.

In a flat, nasal monotone I sprayed the room with words like machine gun fire. I gave them no meaning, no feeling, not even a human sound. It was like being in front of a firing squad with no blindfold and no last cigarette. I just wanted it to be over as quickly as possible.

"To be, or not to be: that is the question:
Whether 'tis nobler in the mind to suffer
The slings and arrows of outrageous misfortune,
Or to take arms against a sea of uh, uh, uh . . . ''

"Trouble," said the agent, who was as offended as he was bewildered.

Stark Hesseltine was not a man who usually displayed his feelings to strangers, but I really got to him. You could tell by the stunned expression on his face. His eyes bugged out from his head and his face burned with slow rising rage. He had this weird look. I guess I surprised him. He had expected me to be good.

"Stop," he said with anger. "It's *fortune*," he sneered, "not *mis*fortune." He was really upset. He stared down at the desk and shook his head as he whispered with controlled hostility, "Get out. Just get out."

I didn't know what to do. After a silent pause I said, "Does this mean the trip is off?"

Suddenly I was Ed Norton and he was Ralph Kramden. The man went ballistic. "Get out of here!" he screamed.

The rest is all a painful blur. My face turned red and my ears burned with embarrassment. I felt humiliated and disgraced as I marched past his assistant and the actors in the reception area. Up until then I had thought I could do anything that involved being an actor. If you wanted me to play a tennis player you just had to hand me a racquet. If you wanted me to play an astronaut you just had to point me to the rocket. It didn't matter what. All I had wanted out of acting was to feel good about myself. I wanted to be able to say, I'm special—because, I guess, nobody else had ever said it. I walked out of Stark Hesseltine's office and the acting profession forever.

Beverly tells me that I slept around the clock for the first four days after my humiliation and that she had a big fight with me about it in the dining room of the Fifty-seventh Street apartment. I don't remember any of it. All I remember is falling into a deep, dark pit of depression and not being able to climb out. For weeks I found myself sleeping until three in the afternoon and staying up all night in search of a laugh or two. I'd have settled for a smile. Every day and every night I toted a heavy emotional load, like weights on my chest. There was no way that I could make myself go back to a selling job and I couldn't seem to recover from my mortifying experience. It had totally crushed me. If it wasn't for Silver I don't think I'd have ever gotten out of bed. Taking care of him gave me the only reason for getting up at all. I was lost and didn't know what to do with the rest of my life.

Beverly and Alan were deeply concerned and never missed an opportunity to suggest things for me to do that might pull me out of my depression. They tried idle conversation, suggested restaurants, movies, social get-togethers. They did their best to cheer me up and get me back to the person I had been, but nothing changed. We were all so young and inexperienced, and my emotional logjam was beyond the scope of what any of us could handle. There were many discussions about my problem but they all ended the same way. Nothing changed. And then one night we were invited to Michael Hartig's apartment. Although Michael was Alan's agent his relationship with him was warm and friendly. Alan always talked about me to Hartig, who became intrigued with my brief episode in the acting profession. He was in his early thirties then and very bright, very wise for his age.

The idea of being in the same room with another actors' agent made me nauseous, even in a safe social situation. But Michael was and is to this day a person with a good heart. While we sat around over drinks, he indicated how concerned he was that I was not handling my problem very well. Early in the evening, he set his drink down, looked me straight in the eyes and said, "What did you think you were doing in the acting profession? You tried to get in on a pass and it didn't work. Now it's time to move on. You've had a major disappointment, you've taken your lumps, and you've got to get over it. Have you considered doing something else? There's an awful lot out there to do besides acting and selling."

"Like what?" I asked.

"I don't know," he shot back at me. "Find out. Take an aptitude test. You may be blessed with skills and talents that you don't know you have. You might get interested in something else."

He caught my attention with that statement and struck a spark of curiosity in me.

"There is an organization called the Federation of Jewish Philanthropies that offers aptitude tests for anyone who wants one. I'd look them up if I were you," he said.

Although my heart was still heavy I knew he was making sense. I liked what he said and became determined to get myself out of the morass I was in.

I got out of bed early the next morning and went directly to the phone book. I looked up the Federation of Jewish Philanthropies and called them. As their phone rang I could feel my optimism fading away like a candle about to go out. My interest was waning and my energy was dropping to zero. Fortunately, someone answered the phone at the other end before I could hang up. Three days later I went to see an employment counselor to discuss taking a battery of aptitude tests. I was told the testing would take from three to five hours to complete. Two weeks later I returned to the organization's building on Park Avenue South, where I was directed to a room and handed a stack of tests and a box of pencils. My counselor told me that I was about to take the Interest-Aptitude Value Test and that it involved hundreds of questions. Once the tests were completed they were going to be evaluated and then discussed with me in terms of my best choices for the future, whatever that was going to be. It all seemed so remote and hopeless.

I loosely balanced a yellow pencil between my fingers like a straw that was going to blow away any minute and turned to the first page of the test. It was with a tortured sense of gloom that I looked down at the paper. My God, there were a lot of questions on it, and they pertained to hundreds of things that a person could do for a living. The silence was intense but the questions captured my attention more than I thought they could. I sat in that barren room for almost three hours as I checked off hundreds of short inquiries about my interests. There were medical questions, legal questions, scientific questions, mathematical questions, language questions, and so many others, all pertaining to occupations and professions. I never realized there were so many different occupations to go into.

And then I came to the one question that leaped off the page like words with legs and stopped the test cold. *Would you like to train dogs for the blind?* My mouth opened and my eyes widened as I took short, quick breaths. I checked off "no" and moved on to the next question. Then I went back and checked off "yes" and tried to go on. My pencil took on a life of its own and began to erase the "no" and trace around the "yes" marking it black until the pencil point snapped off. Suddenly the words washed off the page like surf and turned into pictures. My brain flashed scenes from my childhood like a slide show. It was all about dogs. Every dog I ever touched, held, hugged, curled up with, walked, fed, nursed, loved, and fought my father for trotted across my eyes at that moment. I remembered when I was a teenager and had had a terrible fight with my father. I had slept on a bench in Central Park for three nights with my dog wrapped around me for warmth. There was Silver and Miss Boo and Smoky, who died in my arms, and all the strays my father had ever brought home who slept with me and licked my smiling face and made me feel like a worthwhile person. Did I want to train dogs for the blind? No. I wanted to train dogs for everyone because I knew that was a wonderful, valuable thing that I could learn to do as well as anybody. That one question ignited a spark in me that quickly became a serious flame. With great impatience I finished the tests, left the building, and headed for the nearest telephone. For the first time ever, it was clear to me what I was looking for. I knew this was it. I just knew, and there was no need to go back for the evaluation. I was about to change my life.

As I was leaving the building I found a pay phone in the lobby with a set of Yellow Pages. After looking through the "Dog Training" section I placed a call to the Captain Haggerty School for Dogs (and Dog Trainers).

"Hi, do you give a course in dog training?"

The voice at the other end was from someone who seemed distracted and annoyed. It was Haggerty who answered, "Yes, we do. But I'll have to meet you first. Get yourself to my place on Jerome Avenue in the Bronx. Do you think you can find it?"

"I'll find it," I said.

I took a subway and an hour later I was in the Bronx, standing in the little office of a storefront dog-training business. The place was deserted. It was very quiet as I stood around for a minute or two waiting for a sign of life. Suddenly, a lot of dogs began to bark from somewhere in the back. They made a racket.

"Is anyone here?" I shouted.

"Wait a minute!" someone shouted back. And out walked this gigantic man with a gruff tone of voice. He resembled a professional wrestler and I must admit he was a little frightening. There I was, in front of Captain Arthur J. Haggerty himself. The captain was a huge, serious-looking man who frightened most people when they first met him. He was six-foot-three and at that time weighed 350 pounds. More than his imposing size, more than his totally shaved head, more than his piercing blue eyes, it was his skeptical tone of voice and suspicious questioning that were so intimidating.

I introduced myself and told him that I wanted to enroll in his dog trainer's course. He informed me that it cost $250, was for five days a week and took six weeks to complete. His interview was tough and demanding. I had to tell him a great deal about myself and why I thought I could be a trainer. What he was looking for was sincerity.

"I don't want to waste my time on you if you're not serious about this," he said in his toughest military manner.

"I'm serious," I said, "but how do I know if I can be a good dog trainer?"

"Don't worry about it. I'll let you know," he snapped at me.

To this day I don't know what he thought about me after I told him about my life and how strongly I felt about dogs. After the interview he introduced me to his two instructors who, he said, were going to teach me all about the basics of dog training.

"Then I'm in?" I asked.

He gave me just a bit of a smile and said, "Yeah, yeah. You're in . . . for two weeks. I'll see how you do by then and make an evaluation. If it doesn't work out by then, you're out. Come back tomorrow morning, eight sharp, and for crissake be on time. I hate people that are late."

For the next six weeks I showed up bright and early every morning because I didn't want to give him a reason to dump me. Besides, I loved what I was doing. I had never been so motivated in my entire life. Two weeks passed and Haggerty never said a word about leaving. I was a hard-working pupil and went on to finish the entire course to the end. It was one of the great experiences of my life and I guess it showed. My schooling took place out in the street with his two instructors and many different dogs for a full eight-hour day. I lived and breathed everything about dogs, dog behavior, dog training. It was great. They taught me how to teach the basic obedience commands with a lot of elegant technique. Both trainers had a soft touch with me and the dogs we worked with. They were polished experts and started me off in the right direction. When I would get home at night, I'd call Silver to me and practice everything I had learned during the day on him. You could say that we both graduated from the school at the same time. When I wasn't practicing on my own dog I'd be reading books about dogs. I even wrote a book report about the Seeing Eye.

Captain Haggerty would come out every day and watch me work with the dogs and then personally show me some of the techniques. There was a lot going on in his business at the time. He was very involved with dogs on television and in the movies and was always working on tricks and stunts. He was without question the best trainer in the business. His background was impressive. He called himself Captain Haggerty because he had been an army captain and a former dog train-

Out walked this gigantic man with a gruff tone of voice. He resembled a professional wrestler, and I must admit he was a little frightening.

ing officer at the Army Dog Training Center in Fort Carson, Colorado. He was also the commanding officer of the 25th and 26th Infantry Scout Dog Platoons. His military background with dogs is as extensive as his civilian background. But it was his involvement in show business that made him so interesting. As a result of training hundreds of dogs for TV and movies he began to perform with the dogs and has become something of a legend as a character actor in his own right. The Captain has personally appeared in more than twenty movies and was a regular on the David Letterman show and a guest on many other television shows. For me, his greatest credit was his school for dog trainers. While I was his student, many people hired him to train their new dogs. Watching him work was one of the most important learning experiences I ever had. Captain Haggerty was a master. To look at him, you'd think he'd eat any dog that gave him a hard time. But he was a man of incredible gentleness and sensitivity with dogs despite his great size and tough pose. He could train a Toy Poodle with the same ease and comfort as any large, formidable German Shepherd. As a matter of fact, his personal dog in those days was a dainty little Chihuahua that went everywhere with him inside his coat pocket. What a picture the two of them made.

Although I had much to learn, I was well on the road to becoming a professional dog trainer by the time I finished the course. I read everything about dogs that I could get my hands on. Unfortunately, there wasn't too much available at the time. Haggerty kept putting books in my hands and I would devour them on the long subway ride to and from his school. I stayed up many nights reading about all the breeds from the *Complete Dog Book* of the American Kennel Club. I read Blanche Saunders's *The Complete Book of Dog Obedience* and her *Training You to Train Your Dog.* I also read books by James Lamb Free, William Koehler, Clarence Pfaffenberger, and a number of others.

I finished my course with Haggerty in May 1968. Immediately afterward I answered an ad from a company that was looking for dog trainers and was hired on the spot. I quit, however, after two months because I soon realized the company didn't care whether their clients' dogs were trained properly or not. In July of that year Beverly and I were married and Alan Feinstein was my best man. It was then that I struck out on my own and started my own company, the National Institute of Dog Training, which in the beginning consisted of a wall phone in my kitchen and an old Volkswagen. I was successful from the very beginning. Most of the dogs I trained liked me, many even loved me. Being trained by Arthur Haggerty was an important part of it but so was being raised with dogs all my life and so was loving them so much. I finally had my own dream and it had miraculously come true from the moment of its inception.

chapter six

the write way to train

A trainer I knew once expressed admiration for my ability to get dogs to love me so quickly. Ten seconds is all it usually takes. Most of the dogs I meet are eager to please me and accept training. I've been able to do that almost from the beginning. It could be the high-pitched baby talk I use or it could be the instant bonding techniques that just come naturally to me. There's always something going on between the dog I'm working with and me. I suppose it's a gift. Once that magic thing clicks between me and the dog I become free and loose and I'm able to make it work for both of us. I love it. It is a source of great pleasure for me and I think that is what I communicate.

The dogs I train share my enthusiasm and appreciation for that something special that exists between us. The results I get come from something more than dog training techniques; they are from understanding what they understand, feeling what they feel, seeing what they see. The easiest thing for me is to see the world from a dog's point of view. I have often been asked about my training techniques and where I learned them. Of course, there were the basics from Captain Haggerty, but over the past twenty-five years I have gone well beyond that.

I've been fortunate enough to have the opportunity to try different ways to train dogs and experiment with new ideas and concepts that I either created myself, read about or learned from other professionals. Experience has taught me that new techniques, even those that get results, are not necessarily good simply because they are new or different. My guiding rule is this: Everything I do has to be from the point of view of the dog I'm working with at the time. I ask myself, how would I feel about this if I were that dog. Of course, the answer to the question must take into account what's known about natural *dog* behavior and not *human* behavior. However, the techniques that I use must also be good for the pet owner. But it wasn't always that clear. When I first went out on my own as a dog trainer I had an awful lot to learn.

Oh, my god, Beverly, we're a success.

Early in the game I was the entire training staff of the National Institute of Dog Training and Beverly was the entire administrative staff. We started the business with an ad in the dog section of the *New York Times* and held our breath. Happily, it didn't take long for the calls to come in from first-time dog owners looking for help with their new pets. There were six calls in the first week and I did eleven hundred dollars' worth of business.

"Oh, my God, Beverly, we're a success," I shouted as we jumped around the living room of our tiny apartment.

What I offered was a six-week obedience course in the owner's home and I charged between $145 and $225, depending on my evaluation of the dog and how difficult it was going to be to train it. I also offered to come back any time during the life of the dog and retrain it if it became necessary. It was a good deal. (I charge considerably more these days.) What I didn't realize at the time was that I was one of a very few professionals training dogs in the home. It was a new concept at the time.

My very first call came from a young couple in Scarsdale with a high-energy Weimaraner who liked to jump a lot, mostly on people. When I told them about Silver, my Weimaraner, we began swapping chewing stories. We became soulmates of destruction. In the first half hour I was able to get their dog to stop jumping and learn to Sit and Stay and they were pleased enough to sign a contract for $165. I remember speeding back to Manhattan and excitedly running into the apartment with a bottle of wine to celebrate our first contract. We were off to the races.

Looking back at that moment I remember feeling so confident that I could train that crazy Weimaraner and change his problem behavior. It was a great feeling. The dog was very responsive and had learned everything by the third week. I was then able to spend the rest of the time teaching the dog's owners how to handle him and execute the obedience commands. By the time I left them, they had a very well-trained dog and they were pretty good themselves.

Even though being on my own was much more demanding and a little scary, it felt great. I had to screen each call myself, evaluate the client's dog and then sell the concept of dog training along with my ability to do the job. My past experience in selling served me well. Working for a large dog training company for two months gave me just enough experience to understand that I was a *natural* and was among those who had found their life's work.

One of my earliest training jobs was from a lady in Harlem who saw my ad in the Sunday paper and called early the next morning. She owned a dance club and wanted to have her dog trained.

"Do you do obedience *and* guard dog training, Margolis?" Her voice was very gruff and demanding.

"Yes, I do. I do everything," I answered with a false confidence. "Would you like me to come up and take a look at the dog?"

The truth was I had only *watched* some guard dog training when I was a student and had never actually done any. I had read a lot of books on the subject, though, and was eager for the chance to expand my horizon with a new challenge. Besides, I didn't agree with everything I had read and wanted to try some ideas and methods of my own.

We agreed to meet later that morning so that I could evaluate her dog and discuss the details of the job. I got to One hundred twenty-fifth Street by eleven A.M. and found her place easily. It was on the second floor, above several large storefronts. When I looked up I saw two large windows with neon signs blazing out in red, purple, and green. They said, *SWEET FEET. Dance All Night.*

I walked up a wide stairway and got to the front entrance on the first landing. I rang the bell and a woman with long black hair looked me over through the small window in the door. She unlocked it and let me in.

"I'm Sharell Burnside, you Margolis?"

I nodded.

"Common in, then." She was a heavyset African-American woman in her forties or fifties and very good-looking. But there was no doubt that this was one tough lady. I guess she had to be to run an all-night dance club.

I stepped into a large dark space with only one work light dimly lit. Once inside I smelled stale beer and the lingering odor of cigarette smoke from the night before. All I could hear was the sound of our footsteps and the hum of refrigerator motors as we walked toward the long bar against the wall on the other side of the room. The place was actually a nightclub with tables and chairs surrounding a huge dance floor. We sat down on a couple of bar stools and looked each other over.

"Can I pour you something?" she asked, pointing to the whiskey bottles on the shelf behind the bar.

"No, I just want to see the dog," I responded politely. I was a little intimidated.

She said that was fine and excused herself as she disappeared into the back somewhere. A minute later I could hear her walking toward me in the darkness along with the sound of four paws quickly clicking on the wooden floor. When she came into view she was holding a leash attached to a large black Chow Chow that was about eighteen months old. As they got closer I could see that this was a scary-looking dog that would frighten most people just by the sight of it. I had never trained a Chow before.

"This is Mao."

"Mau? As in Mau Mau?"

"Not Mau Mau. As in Mao Tse Tung. This is a *Chinese* dog. I can see where your head's at. This is my big boy. Don't you think he's cute?"

Cute? The dog was a monster weighing close to eighty pounds, which is enormous for that breed. He was a big bag of fur with stone black eyes that hardly moved in their sockets. The dog stared at me with absolutely no expression on his face. He was like a poker player and I was the jackpot. He looked mean and you didn't want a dog like that looking at you for long. If you wanted a guard dog that resembled a small bear, though, he was perfect.

The woman watched me as I looked her dog over with careful reserve. From the corner of my eyes I could see that Miss Sharell Burnside of Sweet Feet, Dance All Night was starting to have her doubts about me.

"Nice dog," I said with a nod of approval.

"Do you have experience with Chows?" she asked with a suspicious tone of voice. "Can you handle this dog?"

"Yeah, yeah. Of course I can. Are you kidding? I'm a dog trainer. If it woofs, I can train it."

"If it woofs you *better* train it. I'm not goin' to waste a whole lot of my time and money on this. You got that?"

"I got it. You're no one to fool with."

"You got *that* right."

I then took the leash from her hand and walked the dog away from her and did some fast turns as I spoke to him in a happy, friendly voice. "Common, Mao, baby. How ya doin'? That's a good Mao. Hey, here's Mao the Chow." The faster I walked with him the friendlier I got and the more he began to look at me with his tongue hanging out with pleasure. I took the dog through several obedience moves, including the Sit and Sit-Stay positions. I dropped the leash and walked away. The dog held his position. Mao's owner was impressed.

"My, my. Ain't you somethin'."

"I'm somethin' *else*," I said with a confident smile.

It was time to test the dog for guard work. I went into an exaggerated crouch and put a mean, threatening expression on my face to see his reaction. In addition I placed my left forearm in front of me like a weapon. I pretended to walk like I was trying to hide. Whoa, horsey. Mao curled his lip, vocalized a low, throaty growl, and took a wide, threatening stance. I immediately broke off the test and brought him back to his friendly self with lavish praise and a few fast-walking turns.

"Sit! Stay! Good dog. You're a nice Mao-wow." The dog held the position perfectly. Mao's mistress was impressed.

"You are the livin' end, Margolis. You're gooood!"

I was pleased but somewhat concerned.

"Thanks, Miss Burnside. I really am a good dog trainer. It's what I do." I began to hug the dog and rub the top of his head with affection. "I also care very much about the dogs I work with and I'm a little worried about your dog."

"What's the matter with my dog?"

"I think he should see a vet right away," I answered.

"What for?" she asked with panic in her voice.

I paused for a second or two because what I had to tell her was serious. I didn't know how to break the news.

"Your dog . . . well, his tongue is purple. I think something's terribly wrong. He could be on his way out!"

The woman was dumbfounded. Her brow creased and her eyes squinted with disgust and anger.

"How many Chows you trained, you fool?" she demanded in a loud voice.

I knew immediately that I said something stupid but I wasn't sure what. Once again I became Ralph Kramden.

"Ha-ma-na-ma-na-ma."

"You tell me the truth or I'm gonna have someone come to your house and throw you out a window. How many Chows you trained?"

With quivering knees and a stuttering voice I said, "This is the first one." My eyes bulged with embarrassment and fear. I almost called her Alice. She shouted at me like an angry schoolteacher.

"Man. Don't you know that all Chows have purple tongues? And sometimes they're even black, I say, black. You hear me?"

"Ha-ma-na-ma-na-ma. Yes," I answered quietly.

She finally calmed down and looked hard at me. She then began to laugh a full, wonderful laugh from the gut.

"I like you, anyway. You may be a lyin' fool but you know your way 'round a dog. If my Mao likes you, then I guess I like you. Purple tongue, my ass! I know you can do the job but you better talk straight with me from now on."

I trained her dog well and she became my greatest supporter. She even recommended me to several other people. I'll never forget that nice lady and her Mao of Sweet Feet, Dance All Night. I never made an exaggerated claim again.

Next to the dogs themselves, the best part of my work is meeting an incredible assortment of interesting people and getting a glimpse of their worlds. Dog owners from every part of society have called me at one time or another. I have trained the dogs of movie stars, street cleaners, doctors, TV producers, shopkeepers, heads of movie studios and TV networks, firemen, professional athletes—people from just about every part of American life. Many of my former clients have maintained casual contact with me over the years. A few have even become good friends of mine. But of all the relationships that have developed as a result of my work, none has been more durable, more meaningful, more aggravating, and more rewarding than the one with Mordecai Siegal, my coauthor and dear friend.

I met him and his wife, Vicki, in Greenwich Village in the spring of 1969. A jewelry maker with a shop on MacDougal Street had a Basset Hound with an aggression problem. He hired me to train the sad-faced, droopy-eared dog who had bitten two people. As it turned out, the dog was developing cataracts and nipped at anyone who tried to touch him because he couldn't see very well. I was out on the street gently working the dog in front of the jewelry shop when I noticed an attractive woman with long red hair watching me. She was in her late twenties and was barely able to control a high-energy Siberian Husky she had attached to a short leash. The dog wanted to jump all over me and the Basset Hound. He was a gorgeous black and silver dog with steel-blue eyes and a comical personality.

The young woman approached me after my session with the jeweler's dog and asked about getting her dog trained. Her Husky's name was Pete and he had a chewing problem, a pulling problem, a digging problem, an eating problem, and a housebreaking problem. Other than that, he was a perfect dog. She wanted to know if I could change his behavior and if so, how much would I charge to do it. I was invited into her apartment a few doors down the street to meet her husband and talk to him about the deal. I followed her and Pete into a doorway sandwiched between two shops and found myself staring down a dark hallway that was as long as a bowling alley. The couple lived on the first floor of a six-story walk-up, in the last apartment all the way in the back. I couldn't tell you what the hallway was like because it was too dark. This was the first time I had ever entered a Greenwich Village apartment with real struggling artists inside. It was something I had only read about.

Vicki used three keys to open the door, which had two conventional locks and a lock cylinder in the center of the door. It was a Fox Police Lock, which was a device that had a long metal rod coming up from the floor and leaning against the door from the inside. I entered the apartment and was amazed by what I saw. Although it was tiny it was nice-looking, compact, and well organized. The ceilings were twelve feet high, which gave their three small rooms more height than floor space. You entered the apartment from their small kitchen, which was weird because the first thing you saw was a bathtub against the wall, encased in a wooden frame. I had never seen that before. There was a stove, a refrigerator, and a spacious corner of the floor reserved for the dog.

If you turned to your left you walked into the living room.

Don't ask me how they did it but somehow they managed to get into that little space a sofa (which opened into a bed), a coat closet, a chest of drawers with a China cupboard sitting on it, a recliner chair, a TV set mounted on the wall, and a walnut dropleaf dining table with three chairs. The main focus of the room was an entire wall, from floor to ceiling, of wooden shelves overflowing with books. I had never seen so many books outside of a public library in my life.

If you turned right from the entrance you were in the back room, which was even smaller than the other two rooms and contained a pint-size desk and chair. You had to go through the back room to get to the john, which was no larger than a phone booth. There was nothing in it but an ancient toilet with an overhead wooden water box attached to the wall, which roared a flood of water downward into the bowl when you yanked a long pull-chain. Their apartment was like stepping into a black-and-white movie from the thirties.

The Siegals were an interesting couple. Vicki was a very attractive working actress who occasionally appeared in stage plays, TV commercials, and soap operas. She was born in Ohio and grew up in Texas and looked very midwestern. Her stage name was Vicki Blankenship, which was her real name.

Mordecai was thirty-five at the time and very different from his wife. He did not fit any midwestern image that Madison Avenue had in mind and he would never have found a suit at Brooks Brothers. He was short, stocky, and intense. His thick glasses, full beard, and thick, black, wavy hair made him look like a radical college teacher or the leader of a band of anarchists. He was, in fact, a writer. I had never met anyone like them before and was fascinated by their unique Greenwich Village life-style.

*Pete was a happy, gentle dog with a
funny personality.*

Despite all that, my impressions of people were based on their dogs and how they treated them. It was clear to me that these two people cared a great deal about their dog and were real animal lovers. Pete was a happy, gentle dog with a funny personality—he loved to yodel and jump in the air with all fours leaving the ground at once. They also had the greatest cat I had ever met. I was not a cat person. As a matter of fact, up until that time I didn't even like them. But their cat turned me around. He was half Manx and half Siamese and was as unusual as his two owners. His name was Max and he was good-natured, friendly, and full of life. He hopped onto my shoulder the minute I sat down on the sofa and looked at me with his stunning green eyes, demanding my attention with his meowing. I fell in love with that cat instantly and have fallen for a lot of others since.

I remember trying not to show how impressed I was with them as I discussed what I could do to stop their dog's destructive chewing behavior and his other bad habits. I convinced them that the first order of business was to get Pete under control with obedience training and then tackle the behavior problems. They agreed and signed a contract with me for $195. Even though they didn't have a lot of money they were willing to spend what they had for their dog. People like that deserve the best effort I can make. I immediately trotted Pete outside and gave him his first lesson as they watched us carefully. What I didn't know at the time was that they were as impressed with me as I was with them.

Once a week for six consecutive weeks I drove down to the Village to work with Pete. I found myself looking forward to this because I not only enjoyed that funny dog, I liked hanging out with his owner. Mordecai made me laugh. He liked interpreting the world around him with a biting, cynical humor that was a refreshing change for me. When I told him that I was going to rent a house near the beach in the Hamptons for the summer he looked at me with disdain and said, "Why do city people spend a fortune every summer for the privilege of sneezing, wheezing, and smashing green bug guts on their legs? The country is too noisy, especially at night. The crickets and the cicadas sound like plane crash survivors crying for help. I grew up in the city. I need to hear sirens and garbage truck grinders and the sweet sound of shoe leather hitting cement. I hate the beach, too. The sand sticks between your toes and makes the inside of your bathing suit feel like breaded veal cutlets in search of a sauce. I'll go to the beach when they spray the sand with Teflon. Besides, I'm holding out for a beach where *people* are not allowed unless they're on a leash. And another thing . . . ''

The weeks flew by and Pete learned to walk with Vicki like a gentleman, without pulling her down the street. He also learned to Sit, to go into a Down position, to Come When Called, to leave the room, and to stop what he was doing, all on command. But I was never able to get him to hold a Stay position longer than two minutes. He was too easily distracted by other dogs, children, cars, and anything that moved or smiled. What can I say, he was a Siberian Husky and was a curious, playful dog with a mind of his own. If you were too close to his face when you spoke he tried to chase the words down your mouth. If you sang in his presence, he raised his head in the air and howled out a song with you. Put a microphone in his paw and you had a stand-up dog ready for a comedy club. Pete knocked me out, and so did Mordecai.

On my sixth visit to the Village I told Mort and Vicki it

was time to deal with Pete's chewing problem. The dog's favorite thing to do was to get his teeth into newspapers, magazines, or books and rip them apart, but only when he was left alone. If there was no paper available he would grab whatever was within reach on any surface. When all else failed he would turn to the baseboards and gnaw on them. The problem had probably started with teething and boredom as the causes. With the teething stage finished and a cat to keep him from getting bored it seemed to me that the chewing had simply become a generalized habit with no real reason for it anymore. Keeping Pete's playful but stubborn temperament in mind, I felt that the best way to solve the problem was to catch him in the act of destructive chewing and give him the strongest possible correction followed by reassuring praise. I wanted him to associate destructive chewing with a strong, emotional memory. I developed a course of action that was tailored to the physical layout of the small apartment.

"Okay," I explained to them, "in order to catch Pete in the act of chewing he must be convinced that he is alone in the apartment. So here's the plan. First, drill a small hole in the middle of the door that separates the back room from the kitchen and insert one of those small, metal peepholes in it. On D-Day I want Mordecai to leave the house at nine in the morning, making sure that Pete sees him go, and have him meet me around the corner. Vicki, you then take Pete out for his morning walk and disappear in the opposite direction. Once you and the dog are out of sight we will sneak into the apartment and spray the room with an odor neutralizer and a disinfectant so he'll have trouble detecting our presence. We will silently hide in the back room with the door closed. Naturally, we don't want him to know we're there.

"Vicki, you return with Pete to the apartment no earlier than nine-fifteen and go out again, leaving the dog in the kitchen. I want Pete to think he is alone in the apartment. Do *not* remove the leash and collar from his neck. Go have breakfast at a coffee shop and stay there until it's over. We'll come and get you. Of course, we have to leave plenty of newspapers and books on the kitchen floor for Pete to chew on. All we have to do is watch him through the peephole and wait. Once he starts chewing the papers I will burst out of the room, yell *no!* in a loud, angry voice and jerk his leash hard to the side. It's going to startle him. I will then reassure him with a few *good dogs* and *attaboys*. This is a strong correction and it should cure him of his chewing problem."

Mordecai and Vicki reluctantly agreed to go along with the plan even though they thought it was bizarre. They were skeptical and very amused by it which annoyed me. I thought it was a good idea and was convinced it would work. I had used the same procedure on Silver and successfully stopped his destructive chewing. Of course, that was *after* he had destroyed Alan's entire record collection.

Everything went according to plan on the day we went into action. The peephole was drilled, and we all played our parts like secret agents. It was fun. When Vicki returned to the apartment with Pete, Mordecai and I were already hidden in the back room. Our eyes were tearing and my skin itched from the disinfectant and odor neutralizer that we generously sprayed everywhere. The place reeked of it. Vicki couldn't wait to get out of there and have her breakfast. She left the dog alone, leaving his leash and training collar on. The kitchen floor had a neat pile of newspapers and books stacked near the refrigerator so that we could see it from the peephole.

Nothing happened. The dog plopped down in his corner, out of sight, leaving us standing in the darkness for what seemed like forever as we struggled to be patient and quiet. Just as we thought the whole thing was going to be a stupid flop, Pete got up and walked over to his water bowl and took a few slurps. He came into view and I could see him look around the room as if he were searching for something, and then he plopped down next to the pile of newspapers. We both surged with impatient anticipation. I don't know how we avoided being heard by the unsuspecting dog. Mordecai wanted to take a peep and I resisted at first but had to agree. If the dog heard him it would have blown the whole caper. When he saw the dog lying on the floor with his chin on top of the newspapers he started to silently giggle with childish excitement. He struggled to control himself. His giggles changed to titters, which evolved into chortles and, finally, uncontrollable laughter with *almost* no sound at all. He looked like a drowning man. He almost choked on his own suppressed laughter. The only light in the room came from the tiny peephole and we kept bumping into each other and each time we did we lost a little more control. The laughter was like a contagious disease. The two of us stood there at the peephole, silently giggling and laughing in the dark like ten-year-olds peeing in the toilet at the same time. We were losing it.

Finally, Pete lifted his chin off the papers and delicately placed a single page between his teeth, gently tearing it as if he were cutting out an article for safekeeping. He then slid the paper into his mouth and chewed it into a wad which became a classic spitball. He then rose to his feet, dropped the disgusting wad from his mouth and went to town on the pile. With playful fighting stances and low, throaty growls he began attacking the papers with fury, ripping, tearing, chewing, and scraping the stack with his paws. It seemed to have become his enemy. The moment of truth had come. I looked at Mort, nodded my head, and furiously threw open the door with a frightening bang.

The dog froze as he looked at me with utter disbelief and amazement. He couldn't believe that I was there, piercing him with my eyes as I shouted, "*no!*" Pete's mouth hung open as an entire page from the *New York Post* slid off his lips, leaving only a jagged patch of a want ad stuck to his nose. I grabbed the end of his leash and jerked it firmly to the side without realizing that he was uncontrollably peeing all over the kitchen floor. As I jerked the leash, the soles of my shoes started to slide in Pete's puddle and I lost my balance. In an instant I fell on the floor and the seat of my pants and the back of my shirt became drenched in Husky pee. Mordecai started to laugh hysterically. So did I. Siegal's Petrov of Alakazan, better known as Pete, skipped through the urine, placed his wet paws on my shoulders and happily licked my face. He never chewed again and I never drilled another peephole. I guess you could call it a Siberian Standoff.

Mordecai mopped up the floor and got rid of the papers as I rinsed my shirt in the kitchen sink and sat down, bare chested, in the living room with a cup of coffee. I kept looking at all the books on the shelves as I thoughtfully sipped from the cup.

"What kind of a writer are you?" I asked politely.

"Well," he answered, "you could say I was a playwrote. I'm just not sure, anymore. Nobody buys my stuff. I do have an agent, though, for all the good it's doing."

Without pausing for a second, without even thinking, I

heard myself saying to him, "How would you like to write a book with me about dog training?" I'll never forget the look on his face as long as I live. It was unforgettable. There was this expression of utter disbelief and something between shock and astonishment. It was all in his face. His wrinkled brow, his open mouth, his squinting eyes seemed to ask how I could have the gall to suggest that the Arthur Miller–Ernest Hemingway of MacDougal Street should write a dog book. Finally, he spoke.

"A what? Are you kidding me? I've got a five-hundred-page novel sitting on that shelf next to two screenplays, a three-act drama, and countless short stories and you want me to write a goddamn book about dog training? Please. Will ya? You're a good dog trainer and a nice guy but, but, but . . ." He couldn't seem to get any other words out of his mouth. I thought it was a good time to leave.

Two days later my phone rang. It was Mordecai.

"Matt, it's Mordecai Siegal. Ah, about that idea of yours, you know, the book about dog training?"

"Hey, look, I'm sorry. I didn't mean to insult you," I said quickly. I liked this guy and didn't want him mad at me.

"No, no. I'm not mad," he answered. "You know, I'm represented by the William Morris Agency and ah, well, I take what my literary agent says quite seriously. I was joking around with him on the phone yesterday and mentioned your idea about the dog book. I thought he would get a laugh out of it but to my surprise he said it was a good idea. He pointed out to me that my work was unpublished, unproduced, and untouched by human hands. He thought a book about dog training could actually get me into print, which is the idea. So, if you still want to do this . . ."

It is possible that I was at his door before he ever finished the sentence. I never drove so fast in Manhattan as I did that morning. Like everything else I ever did in my life, I plunged into something I knew absolutely nothing about. But the thought of me, who barely got out of high school by the skin of my teeth, coauthoring a book was an overwhelming prospect. There was so much I wanted to say to people about dogs and dog training. I wanted to tell them to be good to their dogs, to love them, to train them with kindness and respect and above all, to stop hitting them. I believed it then and I believe it now and the opportunity to say that to a large number of people through a book was about the greatest opportunity I could ever have.

On the advice of his agent, Mordecai and I put together a book outline and a sample chapter. We worked for a month in his tiny back room. I don't know how he did it, but he managed to get the information out of me and put it in some sensible order. But it wasn't an easy process. He had to extract the information out of my head like a dentist yanking wisdom teeth. Siegal often sounded like an interrogator in a World War II movie. "Where are your papers? Talk or I'll have you shot." After a great struggle he got what he needed from me and then threw me out of the apartment. A month later he produced a neatly typed, ten-page proposal with a twenty-page sample chapter. It was the most beautiful-looking thing I ever saw. As I read it he snapped at me, "Don't crease the paper and for God's sake, don't stain it with your tuna fish fingers." To this day, Siegal still guards the paper he writes on like an angry bear defending a cub from predators. He barely allowed me to read the proposal before sending it to the William Morris Agency, where it promptly fell into a black hole.

We went about the business of our lives and tried to put

the thing out of our minds. Mordecai continued writing a serious play about a retarded girl who was molested by her uncle
while I tried to manage all the calls that were coming in for
my services. I was getting so many calls from my ads that I had
to hire another trainer to work with me. Every two or three
months I would call him and ask if he heard anything. It drove

Authors' photo on the jacket of Good Dog, Bad Dog.

him crazy. Sometimes he would snap at me for bothering him and at other times he would purposely tell me about the rejections the proposal was getting from the various publishers. He even offered to send me the rejection letters, which I said I didn't want. By the sixth month the whole idea started to fade from memory and we both let it go. I could tell that Mordecai was relieved. He had never wanted to write a dog book and I couldn't really blame him. He considered himself a playwright or a novelist or something serious like that. Of course, not much was happening there, either.

A year passed since we completed the book proposal. Mordecai was working in his back room, rewriting his retarded girl play, when the phone rang. It was his agent at William Morris.

"Mordecai, it's Don Gold. Guess what I just sold?"

"Oh, my God," he said excitedly, "the play or the novel?"

"Forget that. I just sold *Good Dog, Bad Dog.* Congratulations."

"What?" he said with disbelief. "You're joking! You mean I'm going to have to write a dog-training book? Say it ain't so, Don."

"Mordecai," said the agent. "I sold it to Holt, Rinehart & Winston for an eight-thousand-dollar advance. You're in the big time, buddy. Hello? Hello? Are you there? For crissake. Did you hang up on me?"

chapter seven

heeeeeere's matty!

I don't want to complain, but writing that first book with Mordecai Siegal was like going through the first year of marriage at boot camp. It was a question of personal styles and it took a lot of effort from each of us to make the adjustment. I never complained about his blunt, no-nonsense approach to our work sessions because I was too intimidated. But this was a man who did not hold back his anger. Sometimes he was hard to take. To be fair, though, so was I. He used to get so mad at me and half the time I couldn't figure out why. Working with Siegal was like taking a course in battered bride syndrome. I stuck with it because getting to write a book was just about the most important opportunity of my life. I was just a dog trainer and there I was, working with a real author. Besides, he was usually right about me. Mordecai was the most honest man I'd ever met and over the years I have come to admire and love the guy. He's like the big brother I never had . . . or wanted.

I knew a lot about dogs and how to train them and Mordecai knew a lot about books and how to write them. I was sure that, together, we could create something new and important for dog owners, something that would be meaningful for both of us. I knew we were the perfect team. All I had to do was convince *him*.

Decades later I came to understand that Mordecai's irritation with me was *not* that I'd maneuvered him into writing something he didn't want to write. It was my lack of the writer's temperament. I had never had to sit in one place for many hours before and concentrate on one thing at a time in an orderly, logical manner. After thirty minutes in Siegal's back room my legs would begin to feel like soda bubbles and my mind would drift.

"No! No! No, goddamn it, *no!* I don't want a recipe for pasta and seafood. I want to know where you put your right goddamn hand when you're pushing the dog's ass down with your left goddamn hand. Look, Matt, we're writing about the command Sit. Stick to the subject. I beg you. If you have one shred of human decency in you, you'll do this for me or else one of us is going to die in this room *if you don't stay in focus!*"

"I'm sorry. I'm sorry. I got hungry," I said to him. What I was really thinking at the time was, "The man's a lunatic. I got to get out of here."

It was hard to do what he did. I couldn't imagine it. He would take pages and pages of notes based on what I said and turn it into easily read sentences on clean, neat paper. But the process was slow and tedious. I knew I made it harder for him but I didn't know what to do about it.

"Matthew, you just gave me a beautiful description of one of the many techniques for putting a dog in a *Down*-Stay," Mordecai said in a deliberate, calm tone of voice. And then he squinted and his face began to change and screw up with pain before my eyes.

"Uh-oh," I thought, "Dr. Jekyll, call your service. Mr. Hyde needs you."

"However," he said hysterically, "we are discussing *Sit-*

Stay. You got that? Not Down. Not Down-Stay. Not dogs peeing on your leg. And not the story of that other dog trainer who mimics everything you do, including getting himself a Weimaraner just like yours. I don't care about any of that. Right now I just care about Sit-Stay! Is that asking for too much?"

"The man's anal," I thought. "He's so rigid. How can anyone stick to one subject more than fifteen minutes? He's not human."

Mordecai thought, "He must have a steel plate in his head. That's it. He was wounded in the war. He can't stick to one subject more than fifteen minutes. He's not human."

And that was only the first week. It took us twelve months, off and on, to write the complete manuscript for *Good Dog, Bad Dog*. Mordecai finally figured out how to work with me without committing murder. Each time we got together he set up a tape machine and microphone and recorded our sessions on cassettes. He stopped taking notes and concentrated on engaging me in conversations about dog behavior and training. If my mind wandered or got off the track, as it often did, it didn't seem to matter too much. He could always fast-forward or rewind to the relevant stuff. As a result, our work sessions relaxed and we got to know each other. We began to enjoy ourselves.

After a while, I couldn't wait to get to that little apartment on MacDougal Street and work on the book. Mordecai would often go around the corner to Bleecker Street and pick up a couple of crispy loafs of Italian bread from Zito's Bakery and some prosciutto and smoked mozzarella cheese from Faicco's across the street, and we would make the most obscene-looking hero sandwiches doused in olive oil and oregano. We ate and laughed and worked and sprayed Pepsi out our noses.

Silver, Princess, and Pete, 1971.

Whenever I look at that book today I remember all the fun we had writing it. There was a lot of clowning around, some fierce arguments, and the beginning of a great friendship that has entered its third decade. Of course, after our second book together, *Underdog*, we had a stupid argument and didn't talk to each other for a number of years. We renewed our friendship and our writing partnership in the early eighties and since then we've been closer than before. I think of him as a member of my family. As a matter of fact, he is all over this page right now. We've been referred to as the Simon and Garfunkel of the dog world.

During those wonderful get-togethers when we were writing *Good Dog, Bad Dog*, we would spend about four hours at a time talking about dogs, dog training, our wives, the scary prospect of parenthood, and our dreams of the future. After each session Mordecai would spend the rest of the week digesting the tapes, trying to make sense out of what I said, and then turning it into understandable writing. As time passed the sentences became paragraphs and the paragraphs became chapters and the chapters became a book. It was like magic. Siegal organized the information in my head into a complete dog-training course. He helped me understand just how much I really knew about dogs, which was a lot more than I realized. But he did more than that. The book was also insightful about human behavior and how people relate to dogs. Some of the stuff in the book is really funny. I think the finest contribution he made was to set on paper the ideas and the training techniques in a clear, simple way so that anyone could understand them. He would ask me the kind of questions that new and inexperienced pet owners would ask me. What we created was a book that dealt directly with the needs of the vast majority of dog owners. Back in 1973, when it was first published, it was one of a kind and was located in the Nature section of the large bookstores. Since then, most bookstores in the country have added a Pet section where you can now find dozens and dozens of dog and cat books. That was not the case in 1973.

We never imagined that two very successful careers would come out of that modest dog-training manual, which has continued to help pet owners to this very day. We simply had no idea that a dog book could be so successful. Mordecai never did get back to that three-act play about the retarded girl and her uncle.

When I think about why I've had the success I've enjoyed over the years I have to pinpoint just a few people and events in my life. The love, encouragement, and help from my wife, Beverly, are probably the most important part of the whole deal. Then there was Alan Feinstein's friendship since boyhood. They both have always been there for me. Of course, meeting Mordecai Siegal and writing that first book with him was crucial to my success—but then, so was Johnny Carson.

Several months after *Good Dog, Bad Dog* was published, I taped an appearance on the second most important TV talk show of the time, "The David Susskind Show," and it was very successful. On it the owner of a liquor store appeared with an out-of-control German Shepherd that was extremely aggressive and dangerous. The owner complained that the dog had bitten a number of people in his store and he didn't know what to do about it. I went down into the audience, brought the dog up to the stage, and turned him into an obedient pussycat in less than two minutes. The audience gave me thunderous applause and David Susskind became my most loyal fan. As a matter of fact, he became a client and hired me to train his wife's dog. Unfortunately, the show was taped for future broadcast and we had to wait eight weeks for it to go on the air. At that time *Good Dog, Bad Dog* had been in the stores for several months and we had no indication from the publisher whether it was going to be successful or not. It had come out on the spring list of 1973 and we had completely missed the previous Christmas, when more books are purchased than at any other time of the year. We had the erroneous impression that the book was failing and needed the television exposure of the Susskind show to boost it. Of course, the air date was too far off to help. We didn't know that the book was moving out of the stores at a normal rate of sales and the publisher was satisfied, if not impressed.

I remember sitting in my apartment on a Thursday afternoon with Mordecai bemoaning the far-off air date of my appearance on the Susskind show.

"Too bad the Johnny Carson show tapes in L.A.," I said quietly.

Mordecai looked up and said, "Why?"

"Well, yesterday I trained the dog of a man named Michael Zannella who is the producer of the 'Dick Cavett Show.' He couldn't believe how quickly I could get his dog to obey me and stop jumping all over the place. He was blown away, especially when I showed him a copy of our book. He thought I should go on Johnny Carson and he actually called Bob Dolce in California, 'The Tonight Show' talent coordinator, while I was still in his apartment. He gave me a tremendous recommendation. Dolce was very receptive to Zannella's endorsement and said if I was ever out on the Coast I should give him a call."

Siegal perked up and said, "Why don't you call him now?"

"In California?" I asked.

"Of course. Why not?" he replied.

"Well, what if he wants to see me?"

Mordecai did that hard breathing thing through his nose that was supposed to indicate his impatience. It always annoyed me. He answered, "So? You'll go to California."

"All right, I'll call him," I said, accepting the dare as I picked up the wall phone in the kitchen. Within five minutes I had Dolce on the phone. I reminded him of Michael Zannella's call the day before. He was very kind and pleasant. I told him all about *Good Dog, Bad Dog* and my successful appearance on the Susskind show and said I would like to be on

"The Tonight Show." He told me that they couldn't book me without an interview or audition. However, he said that he would be glad to see me if I happened to be in L.A. He simply couldn't pay my expenses to get there from New York on such a flimsy possibility. Mordecai, who had been listening with his ear next to the phone, whispered, "Tell him you'll be there tomorrow."

I took a deep breath through *my* nose and said, "I'll be there tomorrow."

He answered, "Okay, but there's no guarantee about anything. You're on your own. Call me when you get in."

I told Dolce that I didn't mind taking the chance, said good-bye and hung up. I whistled and smiled nervously.

"You did it. I can't believe you did it. It's worth the price of a plane ticket if you get on, isn't it?" said Mordecai.

The next morning, eleven-thirty California time, I was on the ground in Los Angeles for the first time in my life, marveling at the warm, balmy weather. The first thing I did from the airport was call Bob Dolce. It was Friday morning and nerve-wracking to learn that he couldn't meet with me until one P.M., the following Monday. There I was in Hollywood, the land of my childhood fantasies, for an entire weekend with nothing to do but think about success, failure, and the risk of making a complete fool out of myself.

I had decided to go Hollywood to the hilt. So the first thing I did was check in as a guest at the legendary Beverly Hills Hotel. I was just another gawking tourist as I walked through the luxurious lobby and into the world-famous Polo Lounge, where movie moguls were making deals over phones plugged in at their tables. The maître d' showed me to a table and handed me a menu with a great deal of fuss and flourish.

On a childish impulse I jumped up with excitement, marched to the front desk in the lobby, and asked them to page Matthew Margolis. I then went back to my table and waited nervously as I bit my nails.

A man in a brass-button uniform walked through the entire Polo Lounge announcing in a clear voice, "Paging Matthew Margolis. Paging Matthew Margolis." I signaled the man to bring a telephone to my table, which obligated me to have a brief discussion with nobody on the other end. It was a tacky thing to do but I couldn't resist it. I wanted them to know that I was there, even if it was only for two days. Despite my nerves and what was at stake I managed to fall in love with California. In just one weekend I knew I wanted to live in that incredible dreamworld. It was the longest weekend of my life, but just being in southern California was a great occasion and a sparkling event for me.

Monday finally came and I drove out to the NBC Studios in Burbank for my one o'clock meeting. It all seemed so fantastic that I never noticed many of the details of the drive from Beverly Hills to Burbank, or going through the gate at NBC, or much of Dolce's office, for that matter. I do remember shaking hands with him and handing him a copy of *Good Dog, Bad Dog* and telling him what I could do on the show. Basically, I told him that I could take any dog and make it obedient within one or two minutes. He was impressed and asked if I could really do that. I assured him that I could and invited him to have people bring in their dogs and try me. He said he would think about it, have a meeting with the staff, and get back to me later in the day or on Tuesday.

I returned to my hotel and had no sooner thrown my jacket on the bed when his call came. It was past three in the afternoon; his conversation was very brief. All he said was, "Matthew. It's a go. You'll tape the show this Thursday afternoon, and it'll be on the air Thursday night." I almost fainted. The first thing I did was get on the phone and scream with excitement to Beverly about what had happened.

"I want you to get on a plane and get here as soon as you can!" I yelled to her with nervous energy. By then I was running on nothing but fumes. "I want to share this with you. And to be honest, I need you here to be with me."

My darling wife managed to get her little white Maltese, Princess, and Silver, my crazy Weimaraner, looked after by our friends. She then packed a bag and hopped on a plane. She arrived in Los Angeles the next day, Tuesday, and was by my side early that afternoon. She seemed less impressed with the Beverly Hills Hotel and the glitz of southern California than I was. Her heart has always been in New York.

She threw her bag on the bed and gave me a congratulatory kiss and took a small sip from the champagne I had in the room. She looked at me and shook her head.

"You know, Matty, you're a wreck. You need to calm down and relax. If you don't relieve the pressure you're going to burst before you ever get on the show."

I agreed so we rented a car the next day and got some maps and took a long drive along the coastal highway. It was a magnificent experience. We drove in an open convertible with the sun and the Pacific breeze in our faces. The unending stretches of pure white California beaches are overwhelming the first time you see them. They are unforgettable. We stopped for lunch at a wonderful place called Alice's Restaurant and had an enjoyable meal. The waitress was exceptionally friendly and said to us as we were leaving, "Have a nice day."

Beverly said she had never heard anyone say that before. She knew for certain, then, that she was not in New York. As the day came to an end we pulled up alongside the road, got out of the car, took our shoes and socks off, and strolled down toward the water. We held hands as we watched the sun head out to sea toward Asia. The gentle waves rolled in and out as we watched a horse galloping toward us along the surf. It was being ridden by a young, beautiful woman in a bathing suit with long, flowing hair. The dark brown horse was not saddled and the woman clung to the large animal with her legs. We watched with awe as she rode toward us, passed us, continued up the beach, and disappeared. The day was unforgettable. It was then that I told Beverly that I wanted to live in this fabulous land of sun-drenched palms, horses galloping on the beach, and lemons falling off the trees in the backyard.

"Hmm. We'll see," she said with a generous smile.

In 1973 "The Tonight Show (Starring Johnny Carson)" was an hour and a half long and the taping began at five P.M. A car and driver were provided by the show and arrived at our hotel at three in the afternoon. We were instructed to be at the studio no later than three-thirty. Bevy and I felt like important celebrities stepping inside the car as the driver held the door open for us. I imagined that our status at the hotel went soaring. In reality, no one noticed. No one really cared. It was a common sight at the Beverly Hills Hotel. I don't remember much of the ride to Burbank. I guess I was too nervous. Having Beverly in the car with me meant a lot and I was grateful to have her there.

Seeing NBC from the outside was like a dream. It looked like all the film studios I had ever seen in the movies. But getting inside was like crossing the border of a foreign country. You had to drive through a gate that was protected by uniformed guards and you couldn't get in without being on a list headed *Talent*, which was attached to a clipboard hanging on the wall of the gatehouse. I was so giddy I almost lost control of myself when our driver rolled down his window and said to the guard, "Talent for 'The Tonight Show.' " I couldn't believe he said that and that he was referring to me. The guard checked our names against his list and passed us through. We drove past the huge parking lot and right up to one of the gigantic studio buildings, where we got out of the car and went inside. I was like a kid in an incredible candy factory. It was the most glamorous moment of my life. I felt like I had really made it. Of course, it hadn't yet dawned on me that I was about to go on the most popular television show in the world and talk to Johnny Carson himself and attempt to train several strange dogs in front of 30 million people.

As I entered the proper building, I was greeted by more uniformed guards, who checked our names against another list and had us wait until an escort came out to take us to my dressing room. A young woman, a production assistant, greeted us and walked with us down several very long corridors until we came to a door that had a sign on it similar to a doctor's shingle. It proclaimed, MATTHEW MARGOLIS. It was a nameplate that had been printed, not hand lettered. I couldn't believe they went to that much trouble just for me. Of course, they did that for all the guests on the show, but I was overwhelmed to see my name on the door. The dressing room was carpeted and furnished with a soft chair and a couch and had a small bathroom in it. Against the wall was a long dressing table and chair with a large mirror over it. All around the mirror were soft, creamy lightbulbs, giving it a traditional backstage look. This was Show Business as I imagined it to be and it didn't take a genius to figure out that I was in the big time. Beverly's impression was a lot less romantic. She was somewhat disappointed and expected it to be more luxurious.

I left my suit bag in the dressing room and was taken down the hall to the makeup room, which looked like the barbershop on an ocean liner. An attractive woman in a white smock instructed me to get in the barber chair and snapped a cloth bib around my neck. For five minutes she dabbed white cream under my eyes and smeared my face with reddish yellow pancake. When she finished I looked like a baked yam. From there I was taken back to the dressing room and told to put on the clothes I was going to wear on the show. And then it finally hit me. These people were serious. They intended to drag me out in front of the lights, the cameras, and the audience and feed me piece by piece to Johnny Carson like raw meat. My mouth dried out and my stomach flipped inside out with nauseating spasms. My palms were sweating as I began to realize just how scared I was. My thoughts flashed back to Stark Hesseltine's office and how I'd murdered Shakespeare. Was this going to be one more humiliating experience? Could I do what I said I could? I was about to find out who I really was.

"Matt? You're fine. You're going to be terrific. Now calm down," said Beverly with a loving, reassuring tone of voice.

"You're right," I said.

Somehow, with trembling hands, I managed to put my shirt and tie on and then my gray plaid suit. It was new for the occasion. I sank into the couch and stared ahead, contemplating my public execution. All I could do was try to lick some moisture back onto my lips. After a while there was a knock at the door and it opened. I almost blacked out. Bob Dolce strolled in with a warm, reassuring smile and a cheerful manner. He explained to me that I was going to train four dogs that belonged to various members of the staff. The name of each one was going to be on a tag attached to the leash, and it would also tell us about the dog's owner and his problem such as jumping, nipping, pulling, whatever. I was to come on stage from behind the curtain after they introduced me, walk to Carson, shake hands and sit down on the chair closest to his desk. I was then supposed to talk to Johnny and tell him some funny stories about some of my experiences. "*Talk to Johnny!*" I screamed to myself. "Oh, my god."

"After that," Dolce continued, "we'll take a commercial break, and when we come back you and Johnny will walk out to the playing area and bring out the dogs, one at a time, and work with them." He could see that I was nervous and said, "Don't worry about a thing. You're gonna be great. Just be yourself," he added gently.

"And who is that?" I asked. Beverly laughed nervously.

Ten minutes before five in the afternoon, Beverly and I were escorted to the Green Room, a lounge not far from the studio area where guests were asked to wait and relax before going on. The pressure was unbearable. I felt like I was about to witness my own execution on television. They asked me if I wanted to see the four dogs and I said no. I wanted the segment to be completely spontaneous. I thought that was important for the sake of my credibility. I remember wondering if I looked all right. In 1973 we wore wide-lapeled suits, bell-bottom pants, long sideburns, and slightly longer hair. These days it makes me wince and cringe to look at pictures of myself from that time.

The Green Room was loaded with coffee urns, large platters of food, and several color TV monitors so you could see the show as it was being taped. Suddenly, without warning, I heard "The Tonight Show" theme music strike up and then Ed McMahon's voice.

"Frooooooom Hollywood. 'The Tonight Show' starring Johnny Carson. This is Ed McMahon along with Doc Severinsen and the NBC Orchestra inviting you to join Johnny and his guests . . . Rich Little, Helen Reddy, Cornell University astronomer Carl Sagan, and trainer of dumb dogs Matthew Margolis. And now, heeeeeere's Johnny!"

The music went up, there was an extended round of highly spirited applause, and out from behind the multicolored curtain stepped the most famous show business personality of his time, Johnny Carson. Ed McMahon shouted his customary, "Hi-yo," as the audience screamed and hollered back at him. Carson went through his famous opening monologue. I remember a lot of funny remarks and laughter in response to them. As he got one laugh after another I unexpectedly heard my name come up when the audience laughed at the sound of dogs barking backstage. He explained to the crowd that he had a bunch of "dumb dogs" on the show and that Matthew Margolis was going to come out and show the audience how to teach dogs who can't do anything some basics. I almost choked on a cup of water when I heard my name. He told them that I was going to train the dogs that belonged to members of the staff in a very short period of time. He said the dogs were so dumb they had to be taught how to bark.

The monologue continued as two production assistants came for me, took me by the hand and led me down the hall to the enormous studio area. Beverly stayed behind in the Green Room and waved good-bye to me.

"Matty," she said, "I love you."

I smiled and nodded as we walked away, leaving her behind. All I could do was follow the two in front of me like a condemned man on his way to the gas chamber. As we approached the large studio the lights got brighter and the sounds of the audience grew louder and dangerously closer. And then I got my first glimpse of the performing area. There were hundreds of blazing lights from every square inch of the ceiling and along the walls in addition to miles of thick black cables all over the floor of the backstage area. And then I saw it. There it was, the famous stage set so familiar to most of America with Carson's desk on a platform and the row of plush chairs next to it. Facing the set was the large audience, hundreds of people sitting in rows of theater seats that were raked upward. There was electricity in the air. The place was mobbed with noisy people, laughing and giggling and expecting to be entertained. Out front were the cameras and a small army of production people ready to make it all happen. More people were going to watch me train dogs that night than I could ever imagine. Johnny Carson was already at the desk talking to Ed McMahon. It was all so dreamlike.

They led me backstage, behind the big curtain. The area was loaded with stagehands and technicians. Two guys were standing at the center of the curtain, waiting to pull it open between the pink and the blue panels at the moment of truth. Sweat started to pour off my forehead and my hands. I could feel my heartbeats.

"What happens," I thought, "if the audience doesn't listen to me or if I can't talk or if the dogs don't respond to me?" My fearful thoughts were interrupted by someone, god knows who, telling me that I was the first guest of the evening and that when I heard myself being introduced to calmly walk out on the stage, smile and go directly to the desk and shake hands with Johnny and Ed and sit down. As I stood in semi-darkness behind the curtain, I could hear Carson and McMahon setting up my introduction. They made a few comments about how difficult it was to train dogs despite the fact that they owned many dogs and loved them a lot. And then Carson said my name. I felt like a dog who listens to its master jabber away until he hears the one or two words he understands, like *sit* or *Do you want to go out* or Would you welcome, please, Matthew Margolis.

It had come, the moment to do or die. Funny, though, I lost all control of my actions. Like a boulder rolling downhill, I stepped out in front of the curtain, smiled at the audience, turned to the desk, and walked toward Johnny Carson and Ed McMahon with my arm extended to shake hands as if I'd been doing it all my life. As I approached the platform I suddenly knew that everything was going to be all right and that my life at that very moment was changing profoundly.

I shook hands with Johnny and then with Ed and sat down in the first chair. What a thrill! It was an exquisite moment. Johnny couldn't have been nicer and more helpful. The way he handled his guests was pure brilliance. Like so many others before me, he made me feel so secure throughout the segment that I never once felt I would fail or that I would look or sound bad. He gave me the feeling that he wanted me to do well and did everything he could to make my part of the show come off properly. He asked why people felt so inept about getting their dogs to do anything. My answer was simple. "They don't know how." The audience laughed when he said that could cause problems.

We talked about people treating their dogs like human beings instead of dogs and how the kind of human names they give their dogs, like Morris or Irving, proves this. I explained how I go to the homes of my clients and train their dogs there and that the teaching extends to the dogs' owners. This led to a discussion about housebreaking.

"It's funny," I said. "It's such a tender subject, especially when people call me and tell me that their dog is not house-broken. I ask them how long have they had the dog and they may answer, 'Three years.' I'll ask, 'Why did you wait so long?' and they'll say, 'I thought he would get better.' " The audience enjoyed that.

I continued, "Not too long ago I asked one woman, 'What does your dog do?' She answered, 'Poofie makes chocolates in the house.' " The audience howled and Johnny almost fell off his chair with laughter. He then asked about what other euphemisms there were regarding housebreaking dogs.

"Horace left gifts," I added quickly, trying to control my own laughter.

"Horace left gifts?" he asked. "I had a dog like that. Every day was Christmas for my dog." Roaring laughter came from the audience.

"One woman," I continued, "told me that her Maxwell left surprises. Then it's eh-eh, ca-ca, wee-wee. They just won't say what it is."

I mentioned how the average dog can be housebroken in about three days if people know what to do. Carson indicated that all this stuff about dog behavior and training interested him very much. You could tell he meant it by the nature of the questions he asked. He wanted to know whether dogs understood words or whether they associated words with rewards or actions. He seemed to grasp the concepts of dog training as I explained them. Of course, I told him that dogs understand words combined with rewards. They understand corrections and actions, but the rewards consist of praise and love. We discussed how talking to dogs in long sentences instead of one-word commands was a bad idea, and the mistake of talking to dogs as if they understood the English language.

He then carefully eased the conversation into the teaching process for dogs, especially older dogs. This led us to the dogs that were eagerly waiting backstage. He said they were going to break for a commercial and when they came back we were going to try to put these theories to the test with real dogs. He turned to me just before the break and said, "I hope this works, Matthew. We'll be right back." I laughed but his parting statement gave me a frightening jolt. I wanted it to work, too. The bright stage lights suddenly went out and the production staff milled about waiting for the commercials to end. The audience buzzed with dozens of conversations as technicians cleared the stage area. Throughout the commercial break Doc Severinsen conducted the band through several up-tempo arrangements. During the break we got into a brief discussion about neurotic dogs and I mentioned that they do exist but that it's humans that make them neurotic. Suddenly the stage lights came up again to full intensity and the crew got back to their positions. Someone from behind the cameras said, " . . . and four, three, two, one . . . we are back!" The red light on the camera came on, indicating it was live again. The band then played a few last bars of music and stopped on a crescendo from Severinsen's trumpet. Johnny looked into the

woof!

camera and said, "All right, we're talking with Matthew Margolis."

He went on with the discussion about neurotic dogs briefly and then rose from his chair, indicating that I should do the same. We both walked to the front of the colored-paneled curtain in the stage area and began to speak. He asked for the first dog and the curtain parted. A large, white mixed breed resembling a sheepdog trotted out to the center of the stage. The audience laughed at how frisky the dog behaved. Johnny reached for a tag attached to the leash and read it to the audience. He informed them that the dog's problem was its name, which was Dudley Rodney Wellington Bernstein. The tag said that the dog does anything he wants to and never listens.

I took the leash from Johnny and walked the dog back and forth around the stage. At last, I had a chance to do what I do best, train dogs.

"Common, Dud," I said as I walked the dog quickly around the stage, taking charge of his behavior. "Now what I'm gonna try to do is teach Dudley to Sit, come on, Dud, and to Heel and maybe to Stay in about two minutes. Come on, Dud. Come on, buddy. Hi! Come on, buddy. Hit it!" By pulling up on the leash and pushing the dog down on the rear end I got the dog into a Sit position.

"Stay! Much better." The dog tried to move out of the position. "No! SSSss. Stay." The dog then remained in the proper position. "Good boy. Stay."

I started walking back and forth in front of the dog, capturing his attention like a snake charmer, and then around the dog from his rear. At one point I raised one leg over his head. Trying to keep his focus on me instead of the moving

138

camera and the noisy audience. I whimpered like a crying puppy. It is a technique I use to get the dog's attention but, at the same time, keep him in a Sit-Stay.

"Are you all right, Matt?" asked Carson, going for the laugh and getting it.

I tried to smile as I concentrated on teaching this dog to hold his position with a Stay command. Johnny Carson's comedy, audience reactions, camera movements, and wisecracks from the band made it difficult to teach the dog at the same time. It was quite a challenge.

"What you really try to do is make him aware of you," I explained to Carson. It pleased me to see the dog hold the Sit-Stay without moving even after more whimpering from me.

"Attaboy," I said. The audience spontaneously burst into loud applause. The dog, in the Sit position with his back to them, turned his head around to see where the applause was coming from. He was really cute.

I then explained the techniques for teaching Sit and how to use the leash and collar.

"You pull up on the leash and collar and push his hind quarters down," I said, "and you tell him to Sit." I pointed to Dudley as I said this and the dog went right back into the Sit position and held it. With dramatic flair I then dropped the leash from my hand and walked away. The dog never moved, causing the audience to applaud with great enthusiasm. The sequence impressed Carson, I could tell.

"You never worked with the dog before?" he asked with incredulity.

"I never saw him before in my life."

I gave the dog the command Stay and then walked a few feet away from him and knelt down. In a very excited, happy tone of voice I clapped my hands and said, "Okay, Mr. Dudley." The dog ran to me happily, shaking his rear end with pleasure. I scooped him up in my arms like a baby and kissed him on the nose. I then put the dog down and handed the leash to Johnny, who gave him to someone backstage.

The next dog to come out on stage was a small, fat terrier mix who belonged to the show's stage manager. The dog's name was Looey and the tag on his leash said he developed sexual attachments to humans. I handed the leash back to Johnny and said, "Why don't *you* work him?" Carson's lightning ability to get a laugh where there was none prompted him to say, "What do you *mean*, work him?" The audience screamed with laughter at the sexual innuendo as he took the leash from me. After one or two other funny remarks he began to imitate my training techniques of walking back and forth in front of the dog. Of course, he exaggerated the movements and played them for laughs. He kept telling the dog to Sit. He must have said the word ten times until the dog finally did it for him. The audience cheered and applauded him. He then attempted to get the dog to Stay with an exaggerated walk around the dog the way I did it with Dudley, making a buggabugga gesture by flapping his hands next to his own ears. He raised his left leg high in the air and swung it over the dog's head. It cracked me up. He kept saying, "Looey, Looey. Come here, come on. Sit, Looey, Sit. There, is that about it?" I could hear myself roaring with laughter along with the crowd. The man was very funny.

The next dog that came out was a large, red-coated Irish Setter type who romped out nervously. The dog wanted to run off stage. He was a strong animal and kept pulling away. The dog almost dragged Carson away. It belonged to Pat McCormick and his name was Alfie. After a few comic remarks about the dog's owner Carson read the tag aloud, which indicated that the dog was goofy and untrainable. "You might say the owner is also," quipped Carson.

Johnny handed me the leash and stepped back to let me do my thing. I began to walk the dog around, back and forth, just to get his attention and respect.

"Come on, Alf. Come on. Alfie, Heel. Good boy." I was able to place the dog in a Sit position after many repeated tries. The busy environment distracted the dog because he was an excitable animal. He resisted as much as he could until I got him in place by jerking him firmly with the leash. Carson understood that it was the repetition of the verbal commands Sit and Stay in connection with the action that let the dog know what to do. Because of his interest in the process he wanted to be able to do it, too. He bent down and called the dog to him. Taking the leash in his hand, he properly placed the dog in the Sit position and then employed the right hand gesture for Stay. He commanded the dog to Sit and then to Stay. The audience applauded. He then tried to take the dog to the center of the curtain and hand him off to the stage-hands, but Alfie pulled him hard to the side. The audience laughed as Johnny allowed the dog to drag him off.

We both walked back to the center of the stage and took the leash hooked onto the next dog, a fluffy, white Bichon Frise. The dog was very friendly and somewhat frisky. He kept jumping on Johnny's leg, trying to get him to pick him up. The dog belonged to Shirley Wood, a long-time Carson Productions staff member. Her dog's name was Dolly—Dolly Wood. Carson got the biggest laugh of the show when he read the tag on the dog's leash.

woof!

" 'Does a doo in the den from time to time.' For those of you who weren't here before, that means leaves a chocolate on the rug."

This led to a discussion that was dear to my heart. I was able to advise the millions of viewers who were watching the show that night that you never hit a dog, for any reason, even for housebreaking mistakes.

"If he has water all day, excessive water, or he's a little nervous he may do that out of nerves. And no matter how much you hit him or yell at him it won't stop the problem. Rather than punish him for what he's done wrong, the ideal thing is to teach him what to do that's right so you will not have to punish him. You never hit a dog. Never. If it worked you'd never have to do it more than once." Being able to make that little speech to the public made my trip to California truly worthwhile.

Johnny gave me the opportunity to talk about teaching housebreaking techniques and how much time you have to correct a dog for his mistakes before he is no longer able to associate the correction with the misdeed. It surprised him to learn that you must make the correction within ten seconds of the mistake or the correction has no value. We talked about using the right tone of voice in giving commands, praise, and corrections, and how it is important that you not frighten a dog you are trying to train. I was able to get in the fact that fear teaches nothing. As we tied it all up with the idea of being patient, the piano started to play in the background as the cue to wrap it up. Johnny thanked me and handed me the little white dog. The audience applauded enthusiastically and gave me the impression that they thoroughly enjoyed my segment. I then left the stage through the pink and blue paneled curtain with the dog in my arms. The applause continued as they broke for commercials.

When they returned from the commercial break Johnny was sitting at his desk again with Ed McMahon. They bantered a bit and then Carson said, "I was just looking at this book by Mr. Margolis." To my heart's delight, he then held it up to the camera. It was every author's dream. "It looks like about the most commonsense book I've seen on training dogs: *Good Dog, Bad Dog!*"

Beverly and I went back to the dressing room, where I washed the makeup off my face and packed my suit bag. We left the building after saying good-bye to various staff members, including Bob Dolce, who were very flattering about my performance. Beverly kept telling me how good I was, although I could barely hear anything anyone was saying to me at the time. I was so relieved that it was over and that I hadn't made a complete idiot of myself. Beverly said she watched the show in the Green Room with the singer Mac Davis, who had wandered in while waiting to tape a show somewhere else.

Our driver found us, led us to the exit, loaded us in the car, and drove us back to the hotel in Beverly Hills. The quiet time in the back of the car was like oxygen. We later celebrated by having a great dinner at an elegant restaurant, the name of which I can no longer remember. We went back to our hotel room and watched the show go out over the air. The experience was numbing.

chapter eight

the grand tour

By the time we flew home to New York the phones were ringing with calls of congratulations from our publisher, friends,
relatives, and of course, Mordecai and Vicki. Many stores had
sold out their copies of *Good Dog, Bad Dog* and reordered it.
Our editor said that the response at Holt, Rinehart & Winston
to my "Tonight Show" appearance was *sanguine* (editors like
these words) and that he felt the same himself. It took me a
minute or two to figure out that they liked it. Of course, hardcover sales would have gone through the roof if the publisher
hadn't sold the book for a paperback reprint shortly after it
hit the stores. The instant the book appeared in its paperback
edition, one month later, the hardcover sales dropped dead.
But we shouldn't complain, because the book lived on in paperback for twenty years in addition to its foreign language
editions and Book-of-the-Month Club sales. Not many books
stay alive as long as this one has. It has entered its third decade
in its revised and republished hardcover edition and shows no
sign of slowing down—not bad for a mere dog-training book.
Not bad at all.

To my surprise, life was very much the same after my tri-
umph on television. Hollywood producers did not try to get

in touch with me and *Time* magazine did not put my picture on the cover. Essentially, nothing much changed. I still had to earn a living and the only way to do that was to train more dogs. For a while my friends and family called every other day to tell me how well I did on the show and what their neighbors were saying. Eventually, even calls from my family faded away. *Good Dog, Bad Dog* came out in paperback soon afterward and the stardust finally settled into a little sprinkling on the floor that we neatly swept under the carpet.

Life seemed the same, but I knew it wasn't. Some part of me understood that things would never be the same again, because I didn't want them to be the same. The phone did not burn up with calls from new clients as I had anticipated and my life did *not* suddenly become more glamorous. However, I did understand more about my capabilities as a dog trainer and how great they could be. What a wonderful feeling it gave me to know that I was really good at something, good enough to do it properly in a highly pressured, public way. It was what professional athletes do. I had returned from California with something more valuable than fame and fortune. I had returned with a good feeling about myself and with a new sense of confidence. It was clear to me that I had the ability to make something wonderful out of my life, something more than I had ever dared to imagine, and I also discovered that I was as worthwhile as anyone else. Somehow, some way, I was going to play the leading role in my own life.

Before "The Tonight Show" appearance and before the publication of *Good Dog, Bad Dog*, my reputation in New York had been growing as an effective dog trainer who loved the animals that he worked with. My message—that you didn't have to hit a dog in order to train it—was getting around. It appealed to many pet owners from all walks of life.

Shortly after I returned from California a distraught man called and asked about my services. He wanted me to help him and his family with their young troublesome Beagle. We arranged for an initial meeting in his home to discuss the dog's problems, what I could do about them, and how much I would charge. The family's name was Heller and they lived in a luxurious apartment building on the Upper West Side of Manhattan.

I remember riding up in a posh elevator that opened directly into their apartment. Beverly and I lived in a very small apartment and it was overpowering to step into one that was so large and distinctive. Although I tried not to have that *gee whiz* look on my face anymore, I couldn't get my eyes to stop whistling. You had to be rich to live in such a place. The immense apartment was in the grand style of old, luxurious New York, with huge rooms, high ceilings, and filigreed borders in the plaster that decorated the tops of the walls. The place was furnished in obvious good taste with a soft, comfortable look. It was like stepping into a four-page spread in *House Beautiful*. What I remember most was the look of brownish wood everywhere. The den was seriously elegant, lined with books along the walls. Even the hallways were special, with framed works of art hanging on every side. The place reminded me of a library. It was the first expensively furnished home I was ever in that did not have wall-to-wall carpeting. Instead, there were area rugs everywhere. I don't know why, but that impressed me.

The family seemed very nice, but I saw very little of them. Mr. Heller was obviously the one I had to deal with. My impression of him was that he was an assertive, take-charge kind of man. He had a strong, compelling personality and was obviously successful at whatever he did for a living. He was also a nice-looking man with a refined, cultivated manner, and I recall thinking that although he looked very distinguished with his gray hair he seemed too young to have so much of it. His family and way of life were perfect by my standards. These were the kind of people you pictured when you read about rich, upper-class families. They spoke properly, looked great, dressed well, had a magnificent home, and probably had a fancy car and summer house in the Hamptons. They had everything . . . except a well-behaved dog. But what made the greatest impression on me was their kitchen. It was the size of my entire apartment. I couldn't even afford their pots and pans.

Like a lot of people living a seemingly perfect life, they had a dog that was making them miserable. The Heller family was plagued by a male Beagle about eight or nine months old who was chewing everything, jumping on the furniture, jumping on people, and having "accidents" all over their area rugs. They were most upset about the dog's habit of gnawing on their expensive furniture and destroying any books he could get his teeth into. He was not a well-behaved dog. I explained to Mr. Heller that the dog needed basic obedience training. Once that was accomplished some of the bad behavior would fade away, and the rest could be easily dealt with once the dog was under control. It was a typical house dog situation, nothing unusual, and easy to correct. The head of the house agreed to my fee and signed a contract with me. Training began right away.

The dog began to settle down and show some improvement by my third visit. The family had taken the training course seriously and followed my instructions quite well. They employed the techniques I gave them for correcting the dog's housebreaking "mistakes" and destructive chewing habits and were starting to see positive results. As a result they warmed up to me and began to trust me and my methods. Mr. Heller told me to call him Joe and he began to call me Matt. The situation was friendly, pleasant, and very satisfying. I began to relax with him once he stopped being so formal. We were able to relate to each other in a more personal manner and chat a bit both before and after working with his dog.

I have a habit of asking my clients what they do for a living, partly because I am a curious person and partly because a personal question makes most people a little friendlier. In most cases it breaks the ice and loosens people up. Meeting different kinds of people and learning about them is what makes my work interesting. Besides, you never know where it leads. Sometimes I barter my services in exchange for something that the client has to offer. It's more fun that way.

"Mr. Heller, what do you do?" I asked as we sat in his living room drinking coffee.

With sincere modesty he answered, "I'm a writer."

"No kidding," I said with childish enthusiasm. "Hey, I'm a writer, too." My voice went up an octave with excitement.

I reached into my briefcase and pulled out one of several copies of *Good Dog, Bad Dog,* which I always kept on hand.

"Here's a copy of my book. Would you like me to autograph it for you?" I asked with naive pride and pure delight.

"I sure would. It looks like a very good book."

"It is," I said. "People really like it a lot and it's selling very well. The stores keep running out of them. By the way, what did *you* write?"

With a serious, deadpan face he answered, "A novel. It's called *Catch-22*. It seems to be doing well, too."

My mouth fell open. He had written one of the biggest best-sellers of its time.

"Then that makes you *Joseph* Heller?"

He smiled and said, "It sure does."

"Oh, my God, I feel so stupid."

"Why should you?" he said. "We're both authors, aren't we?"

I was so embarrassed.

Heller laughed. Then we both laughed as we leafed through each other's books. It was the most enjoyable moment I had as a newly celebrated dog trainer with my name on a book.

Nineteen seventy-two was an exciting, nerve-wracking year for us. We had turned in the finished manuscript of our first book but had no idea what it would look like in print or whether anyone would buy it. While vacationing in the town of East Hampton that summer we met an editor for Stein and Day who, with a partner, owned the local bookstore. He was intrigued with the idea of our soon-to-be-published *Good Dog, Bad Dog*, and fell in love with the title. He asked Mordecai and me to write something for his publishing house. We were flattered. Neither one of us had ever considered the possibility of writing more than one book together. We told our editor at Holt, Rinehart & Winston about the offer and he said it was okay with him because he thought we had already written about all there was to write about dogs. Little did any of us know that between us we were going to write many more successful books. We began the preliminary work for the new book on the beach at Amagansett but did the actual writing in Greenwich Village.

Once again I dutifully marched to Mordecai's back room in that tiny apartment on MacDougal Street and began the process of having my head squeezed by him so that he could transform what came out into another book. We spent about a year completing the manuscript. On this project Mordecai also spent additional time in the New York Public Library and the library of the American Kennel Club digging up research to enrich our writing with information that could help the reader understand the training techniques that I used. It was the beginning of a process that has added a great deal to the dimension of our work since then.

The focus of the new book was how to train dogs that were not purebreds. Purebred dogs have special behavioral

The authors pose for the book jacket of Underdog.

characteristics, and knowledge of these makes training them easier. Mongrels, however, are less predictable. With Mordecai's assistance I developed various temperament tests to enable owners to determine what kind of dog he or she had so that the training could be adjusted to it. It is exactly what professional dog trainers must do. They adjust their techniques to the dog's temperament and behavior patterns.

Many mutt owners believe that their unpedigreed dogs make the best pets. As a gesture to them we made our new book something of a tribute to the mongrel dog by shooting the training photographs in formal wear. So two male trainers dressed in white tie and tails and one female trainer wearing an evening gown—along with four mutts, a photographer, a coauthor and his wife—invaded Central Park, attracting quite a lot of attention. Thus was born *Underdog: Training the Mutt, Mongrel, and Mixed Breed at Home.*

The publisher thought it was a good idea to spend some money on a national book tour for *Underdog,* considering the success of *Good Dog, Bad Dog* and the publicity it had brought us. Also, my connection with "The Tonight Show" had not escaped their attention. They decided to send me across the country for two weeks to appear on dozens of local radio and TV talk shows with as many newspaper interviews thrown in as possible. We thought that it would be an interesting, exciting, and profitable event in our lives. The idea of having a publisher pay all the expenses to fly from one city to another so that you could appear on television and radio seemed like a great adventure. Staying at fancy hotels and eating all your meals in expensive restaurants added to my fantasy of how celebrities lived.

It was a great disappointment to learn that the publisher was only willing to send one of us, and since I was the dog trainer of the team they wanted me to go. Besides, I had already established myself on television with my appearances with David Susskind and Johnny Carson. The situation created a major conflict between Mordecai and me and interrupted our partnership and friendship for several years. We both suffered from the split and have many regrets about it because we spent quite a while going our separate ways. On his own, Mordecai was given the opportunity by other publishers to develop into a highly articulate, knowledgeable expert, capable of speaking for hours about dogs and cats on the broadcast media. When we finally settled our differences, years later, our relationship grew into a deep and meaningful friendship that is stronger than ever before. We still bicker and argue, but with love and confidence in the generosity and concern we have for each other. We are a lot like family.

Stein and Day published our second book in April 1974 and sent me out on tour early that month. Beverly went with me. I wanted the trip to be a glamorous vacation as well as an important memory for us. But even with her at my side, it was nothing at all like a vacation. A promotional tour is a high-pressure, exhausting experience and is referred to in publishing as "schlepping the book." The first part of our tour involved several commitments in New York City in early April, including interviews with *Newsweek*, United Press International, and CBS Radio. Sandwiched between the interviews were TV appearances on "To Tell the Truth," "Midday," "Straight Talk," and "The Mike Douglas Show," all of them now in TV heaven.

In the middle of the month we flew to Los Angeles, where I spent five hectic days running from a number of local TV appearances to newspaper and magazine interviews. I even lectured at a high school. It was considerate of the publisher, though, to put us up at the luxurious Beverly Hills Hotel. As a matter of fact, they booked us into the best hotels available throughout the book tour.

After the five-day grind in L.A., Beverly and I caught a plane to Cleveland, where we darted around town making three TV appearances in the morning, a newspaper interview late in the afternoon, and an evening appearance on television. We were scheduled to fly to Cincinnati the next morning for one day but had to rent a car and drive there instead because of severe thunderstorms. We drove through heavy rain and lightning all evening and were very tired when we arrived. The following night we flew out of Cincinnati to Chicago, where we spent two days promoting the book on the local media. The next morning we caught an early flight from Chicago to Milwaukee, where we spent a relaxed day doing only one TV show and one radio interview.

It was a grueling, draining experience with intense pressure to get to the interviews on time and then back to the airport in order to avoid missing the closely timed flights to the next city. Getting to and from the airports jangled my nerves because the schedules were always either too close together or too far apart. We were unable to dine at a reasonable hour and the nights were spent in terrific hotels that we were too tired to enjoy. All we could do was sleep or watch a bit of television.

We flew from Milwaukee to Minneapolis for one more day of answering the same questions about mutts, mongrels, and mixed breeds. I did the job. I schlepped the book to the heartland along the rim of the Great Lakes, where I talked, I demonstrated, and I trained a lot of dogs on television. With the Midwest portion of the tour completed, Beverly and I flew to Los Angeles for the high point of the trip, my second appearance on "The Tonight Show." When we finally made it to Los Angeles after six grueling days we settled in once again at the Beverly Hills Hotel and collapsed. The plan was for me to fly to San Francisco after my appearance on "The Tonight Show" and stay there for two more days of the same thing and then return to L.A. Beverly wanted to stay behind and visit with her friends. It was a good plan but it was not without a terrible complication.

Out of necessity we left our two dogs behind. Silver was boarded with a friend on Long Island, and although we usually took Princess with us wherever we went, the trip was too long and complicated to do that. She was looked after by Beverly's brother and sister-in-law. At the time they were living with her brother's in-laws in a beautiful home in Hillside, New Jersey. Considering the length of our trip, we were relieved that our little dog was staying with a number of people that loved her and showered her with attention. I remember Beverly giving her brother painstaking instructions about how to take care of the precious dog. It was as if she were leaving her baby for two weeks and it was a hard thing to do. But it was a good situation because everyone there loved the dog. Beverly's mother, who had never cared about animals in her entire life, adored Princess as if she were a grandchild and looked forward to the opportunity of spoiling her rotten on this visit.

We fell into a deep sleep soon after checking in at the Beverly Hills Hotel. The next day, Saturday, I called Beverly's mother in New Jersey to tell her that we were okay and to inquire after everyone. I asked her how everything was going but she did not answer.

"What's wrong?" I asked with an edge of concern in my voice.

"Ah, umm, ah," was her answer.

"What's the matter?" I demanded.

"My daughter-in-law called. They've lost Princess."

She told me that someone had left the door open, the dog had run out, and they couldn't find her. I got off the phone and tried to figure out what to do and how to tell Beverly. Of course, I was supposed to appear on "The Tonight Show" on Monday and was distracted by that. The news was devastating for me as well as Beverly. In the five years that we had had Princess I had come to love her dearly. She was part of my business in the same way as Silver. Clients were very charmed by the sight of Princess and Silver together as they demonstrated obedience commands.

I finally got up the courage to tell Beverly the bad news and watched her fall apart. She became overwhelmed with grief. An hour later she pulled herself together and decided to go back to New Jersey and look for her dog. While Beverly made arrangements to fly home I called a friend of mine at WCBS who knew Princess and cared about her. I asked for his advice and he said he could put it on a wire service if there was an element about it that made it a news story. The idea, of course, was that local papers, especially in New Jersey, might run the story and reach someone who either saw the dog or had the dog.

"I know what," I said. "I'll offer a one thousand–dollar reward for the return of the dog."

My friend thought that would do the trick. A dog trainer offering that much money for the return of his dog was a good feature news story. I sent him a photo of Princess and all the details. He wrote the story and sent it out with the picture to the wire service. He wrote a very clever headline that read: "$1,000 Reward for Lost Princess." It was an attention-getter.

Within a couple of hours Beverly was on a plane bound for New York with red eyes and drenched handkerchiefs. She cried for three thousand miles. She was inconsolable and could not stop. Her brother met her at the airport and drove her to his in-laws' house. Immediately she went out into the neighborhood searching for her lost dog. She walked down all the streets of that community for hours as she called out the dog's name. Beverly's feeling was that the dog would come to her if she was around somewhere and heard her voice. Sadly, the effort was fruitless and nothing came of it. She finally gave up and fell into an exhausted sleep, the kind one experiences after a death in the family.

On Sunday morning she flew back to Los Angeles to be with me for "The Tonight Show" obligation the next day. Even though my heart was not in it I had to go on. It would have been a major setback to cancel my appearance. I just didn't know how I would answer any personal questions about my own dogs, though. The joy and the pleasure were taken away. It just didn't matter anymore. We were completely wrung out from the previous six days in the Midwest, and losing Princess hung us out to dry. With a very heavy heart I met Beverly at the airport and drove her back to the hotel. It was an awful ending to an episode in our lives that had started out as such a happy event.

On Sunday Beverly's brother circulated hundreds of flyers

he had made up with a photo of Princess on it along with the $1,000 reward offer. He asked a troop of local Girl Scouts to circulate them throughout the community, which they did with enthusiasm and goodwill. At the same time, the story that went out on the wire service was picked up by many newspapers around the country. It was especially helpful that it appeared in the Sunday papers, particularly in New Jersey. Still, Sunday was a sad, quiet day for Beverly, me, and our family.

On Monday morning we woke up emotionally bruised, tired, and parched. There wasn't a tear left in us. I dreaded having to tape "The Tonight Show" later that afternoon, feeling as bad as I did. For most of the day we sat outside on deck chairs at the edge of the swimming pool, sipped ice water, dozed in the sun, and tried to pull ourselves together for the show, later in the day. I knew it was going to be an ordeal. At one o'clock in the afternoon we were about to go back to our room to get ready to leave for the studio when I heard my name being called out. My trance was broken. A uniformed page brought a phone out to us and plugged it in. It was my brother-in-law calling.

"Matthew, a woman has her. She saw the story in the paper about the one thousand–dollar reward and called us."

It was as wrenching to hear the good news as it was to hear the bad news. Beverly began to cry and I tried to stay composed as I was given the details over the phone. Just when I thought I didn't have anything left in me, tears rolled down my cheeks and I could barely understand what I was being told. The woman who had found Princess was a housekeeper for one of the families in the neighborhood. She was walking home from work and saw the adorable dog wandering around. Since the dog was not wearing a collar or nametag the housekeeper decided to take her home and keep her if no one attempted to recover her. She was as taken with the little Maltese as everyone else. If she had not seen the story about the reward on the front page of the local newspaper she probably would have kept the dog. The woman was paid and Princess was recovered. When we hung up the phone we just stood there, at the edge of the swimming pool of the Beverly Hills Hotel, sobbing our hearts out with relief. It's a dog thing.

I flew to San Francisco late in the evening, the day after my appearance on "The Tonight Show." Beverly stayed with her friends in Los Angeles. I couldn't believe how many shows and interviews they booked for me on the one day I was there. By the time I got back on the plane to L.A. I had done nine of them. I was riding a whirlwind and it depleted me. I was tapped out. I met Beverly at the hotel that night, had dinner, and fell asleep. The next day we left for home. On the plane I tried to add it all up to see what we had accomplished. On the minus side was the conflict and split with Mordecai. There was the physical and mental exhaustion from the two weeks of hopping around from city to city, show to show, interview to interview. There was the awful emotional drain when Princess was lost because we were not home taking care of her. On the plus side I had accomplished what I had set out to do. With Beverly's help I had promoted a new book in a big way and I had further established myself as a skilled dog trainer and public person. I had also managed to function well and do what I had to do even though I was subjected to intense pressure and emotional stress. Although I feel I came out ahead, a national book tour was not the great adventure I thought it would be.

going west

Silver's greatest pleasure was to hear my command, "Get in the car." No matter where we were, he would run to my car with all his might and jump through the front window, leaping from the ground into the front seat, missing the steering wheel by a fraction of an inch. Then I would say, "Get in the back," and he would hop into the backseat, which he knew was his place to be. Everyone loved to see my large, graceful Weimaraner sail through the air and fly into the car through the window like a cartoon hero. It was Silver's big trick and he enjoyed performing it for anyone who would watch.

I was back from the book tour for two days only to find myself trapped in an interview that wasn't going very well. It was with a prospective client in Ozone Park, Queens. He wasn't sure if he wanted his dog trained and whether it was worth the money. It was a seemingly endless discussion and he was taking up a great deal of my time with his indecision. The man simply had no concept of someone else's time being limited. We were standing outside in front of his house as I listened patiently, occasionally looking at my watch. Silver sat by my side, off-leash. He kept looking up at me with an almost undetectable whine. The dog was getting very restless and the stump that was his tail thumped from side to side on the pavement like a liverwurst with a life of its own. He finally caught my eye and I realized that I could kill two birds with one command and maybe get this person to make up his mind. Things might move along if I impressed him with my own dog's razor-sharp obedience and great intelligence. Silver's performance often helped people make up their minds.

"Silver," I said in a firm tone of voice, "get in the car!" The dog exploded with energy and all the muscles in his smooth body cracked like lightning into a mad dash for the car, which was parked across the street. He was all precision and balance. We were standing about forty feet from the car and the dog cut through the air like a speeding bullet moving toward its target. As I looked at the window on the driver's side I suddenly realized it was not rolled down, and before I could stop him the poor dog slammed into it with a sickening thud. He bounced off the thick wall of glass like a crash dummy and without missing a beat, he turned around and ran back to me, something less than poetry in motion. He sat at my feet staring up at me with his tongue hanging out, looking sappy and seeing stars. It was just another dog thing.

That last year in New York was a busy and exciting one in a new and different way. Our son, Jesse, was born in August 1975, which completely changed all of our lives. Beverly had a new and more demanding focus as a mother, which meant that Princess had lost her exalted position as the baby of the family. She had become an unwilling older sibling in a somewhat larger family that had outgrown its small apartment in Manhattan. The little Maltese was not too friendly toward Baby Jesse. Silver was perplexed by the new addition, although he didn't seem to mind. Our little family started to become a crowd consisting of Beverly, Jesse, Silver, Princess, and me. Changing diapers on a designer couch with two dogs sticking their noses where they didn't belong was not easy. I knew the time had come to make a move of some kind and I couldn't get southern California out of my mind. Business was excellent in New York, though. I'd had to hire additional trainers to handle the constant flow of calls that came in from everywhere. There were times when I had to make appointments for seven days a week just to keep up with it. It was difficult to explain or justify my desire to leave New York. I have never been sure whether I left for reasons of ambition or restlessness or simply a desire for something new and different. It could have been the weather.

In New York I trained dogs outdoors in the hottest and coldest weather. Many of my clients stood comfortably in the warm lobbies of their apartment houses as they watched me train their dogs on the freezing sidewalks, yelling out to me how well I was doing. I remember one Sunday going out on several appointments in the middle of a ferocious snowstorm. All I could think about was that beautiful, sunny beach Beverly and I had sat on as we watched the woman on horseback riding through the surf of the Pacific Ocean.

I never realized how difficult it was for me to do my job in New York until I started to travel around the rest of the country promoting our books. It's impossible to park your car, especially in Manhattan, when trying to see clients. Sometimes you just want to get out and burn it. You have to work in all kinds of unpleasant weather conditions. Everything seemed harder to do in New York. I was tired of the grind. Going on "The Tonight Show" and getting to see California were important experiences for me. I thought, "That is not a bad way to live." After asking a few simple questions in the right places I discovered that there were probably more dogs in California than anyplace else in America, and where there is *woof* there is work. Moving to California and leaving a thriving business behind was still a little scary, but I was convinced it was the right thing to do. I discussed the idea with Beverly, who wasn't thrilled with the idea at all. Her heart was in New York as it is to this day, but she was very generous about my desire to go. We were both nervous because it meant starting all over again but she was my wife, my partner, and my friend, and she was always there for me.

During that period I became friendly with a man in New Jersey whose dog I had trained. He expressed a desire to be a dog trainer and share a dog-training business with me. After many discussions and plans we made the decision to move to California together and start a dog-training company as partners. Several years later, in California, we dissolved our partnership and went our separate ways, but I retained ownership of the company, which is still called the National Institute of Dog Training.

We made our fateful move on Labor Day, 1976, and left behind our flourishing business, our home, our families, and everything that was safe and familiar. I felt like a pioneer heading west across the prairie—only *our* covered wagon had wings and four jet engines. It was a gamble, but I think that my willingness to take risks is something I inherited from my father. It's the most important thing he ever gave me. Taking risks of that nature is something that I just do. I can't really explain why. You might think I do it because I'm courageous, but it's probably more like simple-mindedness.

Three months before our big move we took a trip to Los Angeles to set up our lives. We looked for an apartment so that it would be waiting for us, fully furnished, when we arrived. Beverly Hills was the first place I went to look for an apartment. It was not a practical idea, considering that it was among the most expensive real estate in the world and I was far from wealthy. But I figured if I was going to be in Los Angeles I wanted to fulfill the fantasy to its maximum. Much to our surprise we found a spacious garden apartment with three bedrooms in an attractive, two-story house on a beautiful street in that legendary community at a rent we could afford . . . well, almost. Realistically, Beverly liked the idea of living there because of the good reputation of the Beverly Hills public school system and she was thinking of the years ahead for Jesse.

I also had the good sense to take out a large ad in the Los Angeles Yellow Pages the instant I had a California address and phone number. Taking that ad well in advance of our arrival was the most important thing I did. We started training dogs the day we opened for business. Of course, Regis Philbin helped even more than the Yellow Pages.

One of the major benefits of doing the promotion tour for *Underdog* was appearing as a guest on Regis Philbin's TV show "A.M. Los Angeles" during my short stay in California. It was the highest-rated morning show in L.A. and had a lot of clout with its viewers. If Regis recommended something or someone to his audience, they responded vigorously. Fortunately for me, my first appearance with him was very successful and it pleased him. I was a good foil for his energetic style of biting humor and he got a lot of laughs and audience response out of me and the dogs. His production staff made it clear that they wanted me on the show anytime I had a reason to be in California.

Well, the minute I decided to move there I contacted them and they immediately scheduled me for an appearance in August of 1976. The timing was perfect because it coincided with my first ad in the phone book. From the start, Regis was very good to me. He was supportive, funny, and helpful on the air. He was well aware that I was just getting started in L.A. and was unbelievably generous about it, even when he ribbed me to get a laugh. At the end of each show he would give me many accolades about my training talent. The most important thing he did for me was mention that I was training dogs in L.A. and ask me how people could get in touch with me. I gave out my number and it made the phones ring off the hook. He liked to egg me on. He'd make fun of me, make fun of the dogs, and make fun of my training techniques, which included the whimpering noises I'd make to the dogs. "Matt, do you always talk like that? Hey, I think he is going to the dogs. Maybe he *is* a dog!"

People recognized me on the street as Regis Philbin's dog expert. He thought I was a great dog trainer and used to say so on television. You couldn't ask for more.

For the first two years in Los Angeles we worked out of our home. Beverly set up an office in our spare room and answered the phone, handled sales, and set up appointments. I went to see people in their homes to evaluate their dogs, finalized sales, and did the training. The setup functioned well and gave us a modicum of success, but it limited how far we could go and the sort of things we could accomplish with dogs. I became more ambitious and wanted a larger, permanent place to work. I thought the next logical step was to acquire a full-scale kennel, where I could train dogs by boarding them and thus be able to tackle the more serious behavior problems such as shyness and aggressiveness.

We started looking for a kennel and found one for sale in Monterey Park, a suburb of Los Angeles. It was a boarding kennel called *Dog Rancho* and was owned by a man who bred and showed Cocker Spaniels. The kennel was old and somewhat dilapidated. It had only a small house on the property and many unpaved, gravel dog runs. Despite all that and the fact that it was across the road from a cemetery, the place had potential for someone willing to spend some money and renovate it with modern facilities and equipment. The asking price was fair but steep for me considering my net worth, which, after adding up my stocks, bonds, real estate holdings, and jewelry, was about $2.28. I scraped up every dime I could get my hands on and applied for a loan from many banks, but they kept turning me down. Eventually, I found a bank that was willing to take a chance on me. So with extreme pleasure, some fear, and a big mortgage, I owned a kennel.

The years rolled by, and little by little we modernized the place and established a successful boarding and training kennel with clean, comfortable facilities for 125 dogs, making the National Institute of Dog Training the largest dog-training company in the United States. A lot of publicity has generated about me and my training facility, including articles in newspapers and magazines and exposure on television and radio. In 1986, shortly after the publication of *When Good Dogs Do Bad Things*, coauthored with Mordecai, I realized that the next important step was to begin advertising the company on television. I formed a team of creative people and we designed TV commercials for the Los Angeles–Orange County area. I remember struggling with my nerves during the initial taping sessions.

"Hi, I'm *Matt* Margolis."

"No good," said a voice from the control booth.

"Hi, *I'm* Matt Margolis."

"No good."

"Hi. I'm Matt *Margolis.*"

"Let's take a break," said the voice.

It took a while to get it right. Thank God for videotape and editing. Despite my nerves and awkwardness, every phone line lit up like a Christmas tree the day the commercials went on the air.

As time passed, life just kept getting better. Understandably, Beverly wanted to pursue her own interests and no longer wanted to work for the company. She went off on her own to become manager of an exclusive, high-fashion woman's boutique on Rodeo Drive. Jesse went about the business of growing into a sweet, happy boy, giving his mother and me much pleasure and satisfaction. Believe it or not, the one thing missing from our lives was a dog!

Despite the fact that we dealt with hundreds and hundreds of dogs every day, we no longer had a family dog of our own. Silver and Princess had died after we moved to California. When Jesse was six years old he used to say to me almost every day, "Daddy, when are we going to get a dog? When are we going to get a dog of our own?" And then came Emily, our first German Shepherd.

I have trained thousands of dogs, and in my experience German Shepherds have been among the finest to train of all the breeds. They always excel as companions, as protection dogs, as guide dogs, as hearing ear dogs, as search and rescue dogs, as bomb dogs, and as narcotic detection dogs. You name it and a German Shepherd can do it and do it well. Ironically, I had never owned one of my own until Emily. A breeder was recommended to me who had whelped a new litter of German Shepherd puppies on November 5, 1981. In late December of that year I went to look at them and, after testing them all for personality, selected Emily. I can still see her lengthy tongue hanging out the side of her mouth and her awkward ears, longer than her puppy head, sticking straight up in the air like Bugs Bunny. There is nothing more endearing than a gangly German Shepherd puppy. I remember vividly how she followed me around throughout the entire selection process. At one point I set her down on the ground and deliberately ran away from her. She never stopped running after me. No matter what I did with the other puppies or where I walked, she tagged along. She was a happy, carefree pup that simply wanted to be with me. None of the other puppies related to me in that way. Finally, I looked into her beautiful brown eyes and said, "I guess you're mine. Or am I yours?"

Shortly after Christmas Beverly and I quietly entered the house with the puppy and set her loose, aiming her toward the open door to Jesse's room. Suddenly we heard him squeal, "There's a dog in the house!" She jumped all over him, knocked his toys over, and slurped his entire face.

"Dad? What's this?"

"She's yours, son. She's your new dog."

The look on his face was the one that every parent wants to see at least once in a lifetime. He couldn't stop himself from hugging the little dog over and over again as she continued to lick his face. The dog was in canine heaven and the little boy was right there with her. The first thing he did was name her Emily. I have no idea how he came up with that name but it seemed to suit her well. At first Jesse wanted to do everything there was to do for the new puppy until he discovered the realities of housebreaking, which didn't delight him. He wanted to take her out for walks, which of course was not easy for a boy of six. Like any kid his age, he thought of the young dog as a playmate and, at times, as a sibling. They would wrestle and roll around the floor together and run through the house and outside, making a banging racket as they did. And, of course, he would complain to me that she was nipping and hurting him, all the while laughing hysterically. I tried to show him how to administer corrections and gain control of the dog but it was an exercise in futility. He not only rejected what I said, he ignored it completely. Not even my standing as a professional dog trainer helped. He was too young to see the dog as anything other than another person, equal to him in every way.

Several months passed and the two of them became very close. One afternoon Beverly called me at the kennel as I was getting ready to drive home. She sounded distressed so I asked her what was wrong.

"Nothing's wrong but Jesse is very, very angry. His feelings are hurt."

"What's the problem?" I asked.

"I don't want you to laugh," she answered. "I want him to tell you. But when you get home, please treat it seriously, okay?"

"Okay. Okay. Is everyone all right?" I was getting worried.

"Yes, yes," she said with assurance. "Everything is okay. He's fine. Everyone's fine. He needs to talk to you, though. When he does, just don't laugh."

I drove home as quickly as heavy freeway traffic permitted. The longer it took the more curious I became. Finally, I pulled up around the back of the house, got out of the car, and quickly sprinted into the house and looked at Beverly. She whispered "Hello" and shook her head.

"He's in his room. Remember, you mustn't laugh."

I nodded and said, "Okay."

As I entered the room I saw Jesse lying on his bed staring up at the ceiling and Emily quietly curled up on the floor in the corner. Her chin was resting on top of her pulled-in paws and she had a worried look on her face. When German Shepherds are troubled they crease their brows with uneasiness, just like people. As I walked in the room Emily's eyes lit up for a second and then dimmed like a light bulb burning out. She remained in her slump. Jesse sat up with a somber expression on his face.

"Dad," he said with all the seriousness that a six-year-old can muster.

"Yes," I answered as I sat down on the bed.

"I really hate her. I'm so angry at her."

"What's the problem, son?"

He shook his head from side to side and said, "Dad, she's mean. She's a mean dog."

"What did she do?"

"Let me show you," he answered as he rose from the bed, revealing his four most prized possessions. There, sitting on the bed, propped up against the wall, all in a row, were his four teddy bears. They were much more than toys to Jesse. They were a combination of security blankets and imaginary friends. He pointed to them with great anger and a suggestion of tears in the corners of his eyes.

I couldn't understand what the problem was until I leaned in a little closer and looked more carefully. Then I saw what was wrong. All the eyes were gone. All the noses were gone. There was nothing there. I found myself staring at four blank faces. It was like a bad dream. The faces were somewhat mutilated. You haven't seen anything until you've looked at four eyeless teddy bears. It was right out of "The Twilight Zone."

"See. Look what she did, Dad."

I almost lost it. It was the funniest thing I ever saw. The only thing that held me together was the knowledge that Beverly would kill me if I laughed. Of course, Jesse saw no humor in the situation and was dead serious about the whole thing.

"Dad, what are we gonna do? It's not fair!"

They were inseparable.

Somehow I couldn't sit there and tell my six-year-old son that puppies aren't fair. I told him that we could correct the problem and employ some training techniques so that it wouldn't happen again.

Jesse looked into my face with an expression of indignation and asked, "Is she going to pay for the teddy bears?"

I said, "Well, I don't know if she's got any money, but I'll work it out." They were an awful lot like brother and sister and I knew he really loved that dog. Despite the great teddy bear massacre they remained true friends and close companions.

For nine years the two of them were inseparable. Wherever Jesse went, Emily followed him like a little sister. She always slept with him in his room or just outside his room. Sometimes she slept on his bed or on the floor next to him. She was always with him, even when she got older. The problem was that Emily did not pay attention to his commands. Watching him walk her was to watch him get dragged down the street. She didn't understand the concept that her best friend's dad was a dog trainer and therefore she was supposed to obey him.

When she was three months old I noticed that the dog was sort of hopping around all the time. I had her X-rayed and to my horror discovered that she had a terrible case of hip dysplasia, which is an inherited disease in which the top of the thigh bone, the femur, does not fit into the socket of the hip bone as it should. The result is difficulty in walking, eventually leading to severe lameness and crippling pain. It is a tragic condition because quite often the animal must be put to sleep to avoid pain and suffering. I was not knowledgeable enough at the time to ask the breeder for an X ray of the puppies' parents and grandparents that had been certified by the Orthopedic Foundation for Animals (OFA) indicating that his dogs were free of this orthopedic disease. It is considered a common practice by all responsible dog breeders to do this.

When I confronted the breeder he offered to take the dog back but that was unthinkable. We were not talking about a dog. We were talking about Emily. Fortunately, she was not in any pain at the time. I proceeded to train her like any other dog and live with the condition as best we could. She was so bright that it took only three days to housebreak her. The dog never developed a chewing problem and was completely on- and off-leash trained by the time she was five months old. I did everything with her that I tell my clients to do and to my delight (and relief) my methods worked.

In addition to her life as Jesse's friend she also became very important to me. She was a living example of the perfect dog. I used to take her to work with me on occasion and travel with her to see prospective clients and use her as an example of the ideal dog. She was a demonstration dog supreme. Despite the fact that she was so young, so spirited, and so much fun to be with, she was obedient. She dispelled the myth that you had to wait six months or a year before you could train a dog. Here was a five-month-old puppy that was perfectly trained and fun to be with. Emily always made me look good as a dog trainer and as a person. She was the living embodiment of what I believed and practiced.

In 1985, when I started advertising on television to build up the business, she became the star of each commercial. Some of the commercials asked: "Is your dog chewing? Is your dog jumping? Is your dog pulling? Is your dog digging?" Well, it was Emily that would demonstrate all these negative behaviors. It happens that she would love to let loose and do all those annoying things if I let her. She especially loved to chew newspapers. I would say to her: "Get the paper, chew the paper." On command she shredded the newspaper for me with gusto. As an added touch she would toss the shreds in the air, ravaging all the news fit to chew. What a dog! Another funny commercial she starred in was the one where she knocked me into a swimming pool. On command she would run toward me, jump up on my chest with her front paws, and knock me into the pool. I taught her to do that with a subtle hand signal that no one saw but her. She was more than Jesse's dog. She was my coworker. I had a special relationship with her, too. She was a member of the family and we each, in our own way, belonged to her.

When she was seven we found out about hip replacements for dysplastic dogs with the employment of new surgical procedures. With this remarkable operation it was possible to give Emily a new lease on life. We took our sweet dog to the West Los Angeles Veterinary Hospital, where two marvelous surgeons operated on her for several hours, replacing her right hip. She remained in the hospital for five days and then came home to recuperate. Two months later she was running around again like any other normal dog. It was a joy to know that she would not go through the agony that would have been waiting for her had she not undergone the surgery.

Two years later, when she was nine, our luck ran out. Because Jesse was fifteen years old and away at boarding school in Massachusetts, Emily went to work with me every day at the kennel. It was early November 1990, and I had just come back from lunch when I noticed that everybody was averting their eyes from mine. There was a forbidding silence in the office.

I asked what was wrong. The people in the office said the thing that no dog person wants to hear.

"Emily bloated, Matt." To this day I don't know who said it. "She is in the hospital, next door."

I remember running as fast as I could to get there. My heart sank. I was crying before I got there. Bloat is a life-threatening condition known as gastric torsion, which involves an accumulation of gastric secretions, food, or gases, causing a twisting of the intestines. Few dogs survive it. By the time I got to the veterinary clinic next door to my kennel, Emily was already on the operating table. They worked on her for a while but said they couldn't help. I quickly took her to the larger, more fully staffed West Los Angeles Veterinary Hospital to see if they could save her. I rode with her in the ambulance, holding her, talking to her, trying to control my emotions. I stayed with her most of the night but there was no chance. She didn't make it and died in my arms. It was the saddest moment of my life. I loved her so much.

Ironically, just prior to Emily's death I had set aside the next weekend to fly to Massachusetts to visit Jesse. Although I couldn't wait to see him and find out how he liked his school and new friends, I was dreading the trip. I knew he was going to ask about Emily, and I didn't know what to do. Of course, I had to tell him the bad news, as much as I didn't want to. I took the trip by myself and was miserable throughout the flight. As soon as I arrived I drove to the school and found Jesse, who looked like a young man in his new surroundings. It was awfully good to see him no matter what. There were a lot of hugs and kisses. We were both happy to see each other. As we headed for his room he gave me a tour of the dormitory. I was impressed with the neat, clean orderliness of the room.

After a little small talk we sat on his bed and looked at each other. It was hard to hide my feelings. He looked at me and could see something was wrong.

"How's Mom?" he asked.

I said, "She's great."

"How's Emily?"

"Not so good."

"Is she sick?"

"She was."

All I could do was look at him. An answer wouldn't come out of my mouth.

"Dad, what's wrong?"

"Jesse, I need to talk to you about that."

"She died, didn't she?"

"Yeah."

The hurt slowly spread across his face and he began to cry. He wanted to know what had happened. I explained it to him. He wanted to know about bloat, how it happens and why it happens. I did the best I could but somehow I couldn't tell him about it so that it would all make sense. He wanted to know if there was anything else we could have done or if it could have been prevented. It was a hard reality for him to accept. He told me how unfair it was, and through his tears, he said how much he regretted not being able to say good-bye to her. A little later we drove to Boston, stayed overnight in a hotel, and spent the weekend talking about Emily. It was a sad weekend. As much as we had wanted to see each other, we couldn't get past the fact of Emily.

One week later, after the trip east was behind me, I received a letter from Jesse. Inside the envelope was the following note:

woof!

Emily

Our back door creaked open with the same noise as always. It is difficult to recall bare specifics, but the extra and nonroutine pair of footsteps nonchalantly intrigued my six-year-old mind. All of a sudden, as if it were an ambush, a three-month-old, twenty-pound, uncoordinated German Shepherd puppy came pouncing into my room. I was knocked over easily as she continued her rampage of destruction on her new-found home. My long-awaited dream became a reality as I was awed by my surprise Christmas present, "Emily." This "gift" eventually became my best friend, for I loved and trusted her with all my heart.

We grew up together, side by side. She was my true companion; whether fighting or playing, our friendship and love for each other broke all the "barriers" of nature. Emily was not a helpless, inferior pet to me, for I looked upon her as a sister, a friend, and an equal. In my young, innocent eyes, my dog was human, and she understood me as well as anyone.

As we matured, our unique yet beautiful relationship changed. Both age and time became serious factors as she could no longer physically keep up with me, nor did I have the time to spend with her. This is slightly misleading for we were still able to maintain the friendship we'd always had. At the age of seven, Emily underwent a total hip replacement operation which improved her physical condition greatly. She was loved by our whole family, as she was considered a member, so the slightest problem gathered a terrible amount of concern.

Yesterday, my father came three thousand miles to visit me. When I casually asked him how she was, an unknown frown appeared on his concerned face. Instantly I knew that my worst nightmare and greatest fear had developed into a reality. Emily

Margolis passed away last week as a bloated stomach cut off her blood supply. As she painlessly left, she took with her a piece of my heart, as well as those of my parents. I have never loved anything as much as I did her, and I am grateful for all the wonderful memories that she brought to my life. I dedicate my childhood to her, and I will never forget our friendship.
I love you, Emily.
Jesse

I guess that's just another dog thing, too.

Emily.

chapter ten

the L.A. story

Unlike people, dogs are the same everywhere except for their personalities. They speak the same language, have the same instincts, urges, needs and, in most cases, the same behaviors and misbehaviors. Dogs have no prejudices and are not snobs. When a mixed breed moves in down the block the purebred dogs do not get hysterical and say "There goes the neighborhood." The only dog behaviors that are disapproving in nature concern territory and pack integrity. For these reasons, moving to California and training dogs here is not the least bit different from training dogs in New York City or anywhere else. Of course, dogs in L.A. get to be outdoors a lot more because of the warm weather and because fewer of them live in apartments. My life in California has been everything I thought it would be and everything I hoped it would be. The only real surprise was to learn that Hollywood celebrities are like everyone else, especially when it comes to their dogs. They love them, treat them like members of the family, and will do whatever is necessary to make them happy.

Los Angeles has often been referred to as a company town with one main industry—entertainment. Although that is *not* an accurate picture of this highly diversified city it is true that the creation of movies and television is the town's most conspicuous occupation and preoccupation. It is impossible to live and work here and not come into contact at one time or another with those who enrich our lives with comedy, drama, and glamour. You can't go to many dry cleaning stores or hair salons or restaurants without seeing autographed, 8 × 10 glossies on the walls of well-known or aspiring actors and actresses. I have some on *my* office walls. Those we consider celebrities are simply people like the rest of us who need to come out of their homes from time to time for services like everyone else. Many of them own dogs and, like all dog owners, need to have them trained. Over the years I have trained the dogs of many, many celebrities. I have always found it intriguing to go to the homes of the rich and famous, see how they live, and get a sense of what they are like as people. To be honest, though, I am more interested in their dogs, despite the fact that it is good for business to have worked for movie stars. Most people are impressed and become a little silly when in the presence of famous people and, I guess, I'm no different.

However, I am more impressed by the privilege I have had to pursue a profession that not only affords me a good living but gives me total pleasure. Still, it has been interesting to train the dogs of so many famous people. Of one thing I am certain; the dogs couldn't care less about their owners' fame and fortune, which possibly explains why so many celebrities have them in the first place. The dogs do not know that their owners are celebrities. In fact, in their homes, the dogs are the stars. Over the years I have trained the dogs of many celebrities such as Elizabeth Taylor, Robert Wagner and Natalie Wood, Victoria Principal, Sally Struthers, Rich Little, Kenny Rogers, Michael Landon, and Doc Severinsen, just to name a few.

Among those that stand out in my memory are Cher, Ed Mc-Mahon, Whoopi Goldberg, and James Stewart.

In the late 1980s a friend of a friend recommended me to Cher as a trainer for her new puppy. It was a nice excuse to take that enjoyable drive into the beautiful upper portion of Beverly Hills to see Cher at her home. The upper canyon passages are the hilly parts of Beverly Hills with steep, winding roads that are as picturesque as they are difficult to drive around. They are actually the foothills of the Santa Monica Mountains, which separate Hollywood, Beverly Hills, and Pacific Palisades from the San Fernando Valley. If you fly over the area it resembles a big broccoli with a random bald patch. Beverly Hills is an incorporated city independent of Los Angeles even though it is completely surrounded by it. Behind the high shrubbery and tall trees, surprisingly close to the edge of the narrow roads, are the luxurious homes of many wealthy, successful people, including show business personalities. You can hardly see any houses from the road with the exception of an occasional second-story window or rooftop.

The day I went to see Cher was a beauty, with the hazy sun rising over the hills and the traffic flowing swiftly like water. Driving to Cher's home was an exciting thing to do, even at eight in the morning. It was a great way to start off the day. She is a major star whose singing and acting performances I have enjoyed and admired for many years. After finding her correct address I stopped at the tall wooden gate that kept strangers out, called in through an intercom system, and was given permission to turn into the long driveway. It led to her house, which appeared suddenly from behind thick, tall greenery and, like most of the houses in the hills, was completely hidden from the narrow road. It was a two-story building that looked very new and California-modern, all white and sitting on top of a bright green lawn like a big birthday cake.

I pulled my car into the small parking area in front of the garage, which was around the back, and waited for her assistant to come out and get me. That is how things usually work out here. A young woman introduced herself and then led me around the house, past the luxurious swimming pool, the patio, and inside through the sliding glass doors. It was a beautiful house with creamy white and pastel walls, soft chairs, and overstuffed couches. The rooms were quite large and bright with light streaming in from the windows, which seemed to be everywhere. You could see the entire front lawn from the big picture windows in the living room. Vases overflowed with flowers wherever you looked. Of course, there was a piano in the main room. The house was so tastefully decorated anyone would want to move into it in a heartbeat. I sensed a peaceful, relaxing atmosphere that put me in a beautiful mood the minute I entered the space. It was a very quiet, private world of its own, hidden from view by a thicket of hedges, trees, and flowered bushes, a soothing retreat from the daily irritations of big-city life in Los Angeles. The only sounds I could hear were the birds chirping and the wind in the trees.

After several minutes the lady of the house finally entered the room with her puppy. I wanted to look at her young dog, I really did, but I couldn't resist taking in this very famous person, just to be sure it really was her. Celebrities are used to being stared at and, as a rule, try to ignore that it's happening. She looked different. As I said before, the surprising aspect of many well-known people is their humanness. She was in her own home and felt no obligation to project her professional image for me or anyone else she invited in. It was early in the morning and she looked like anyone else who just got up. She wore a pair of denim shorts and a simple blouse. Her casual manner made an important statement: "This is who I am and I'm quite comfortable being me, thank you." I really admired her for her lack of pretension and for her honesty as a person. It was a relief.

"I'm Cher, how are you?"

She extended her arm and we shook hands. Her down-to-earth manner was completely disarming. Cher and I quietly sat down on a couch, yacked for a while, and then discussed her concerns for her dog and what I could do about them. She had an Akita puppy with a brindled coat (darker hairs forming bands on bright tan fur) and unusual white markings on the legs. The dog was more than five months old and somewhat shy and aggressive. He was having housebreaking accidents around the house, jumping on people, chewing destructively, and digging up the lawn. He was a fairly normal, mischievous Akita puppy. Unfortunately, the dog was unusually aloof and very stubborn. I recommended training him at my kennel because I thought he needed to be socialized in a busy environment with lots of people around, but Cher wanted him trained at home. Eventually, she agreed with me and placed him in the kennel for training, as I had originally suggested.

My respect for her grew enormously because she went to a lot of trouble just to drive out to the kennel in Monterey Park to visit her pup on a number of occasions, like any other concerned dog owner. She was very involved with the process and called us several times to find out how her dog was doing and what progress he was making. The Akita stayed with us for six weeks and in that time she visited him on three occasions. Whenever she came to the kennel she was very friendly and nice to my entire staff. Everyone liked her and tried hard to please her. If her name hadn't been Cher you would've thought of her as just another loving dog owner.

Ed McMahon was living in Beverly Hills in January of 1990 and called me to his home to discuss training two Golden Retriever puppies. They were approximately five months old at the time. Johnny Carson's famous sidekick called *me* because I had appeared on "The Tonight Show" four times and because I had trained the dog of the show's band leader, Doc Severinsen. The young dogs were digging up McMahon's beautiful lawn with a vengeance and systematically destroying it. The dogs were kept outdoors a lot because his attractive house was not the kind of place he wanted to have rambunctious golden puppies tearing through. They were only allowed to be in the kitchen or outside, where they ran around the grounds out of control. The atmosphere in that house was quite chaotic at the time because they were in the middle of renovations with workmen everywhere. They were very noisy and the phone never stopped ringing. In addition to obedience training, Ed wanted me to help him design an enclosed dog run of some kind so that the puppies could play outside without destroying the landscaping.

These were sweet and lovable but rowdy Golden Retrievers and their behavior was typical for their age. In hindsight, he shouldn't have gotten this breed, considering the house he was living in at the time. You have to be willing to accept the physical antics and possible consequences of good-natured dogs that are energetic.

Ed smiled warmly and said in a desperate yet cheerful tone, "Matt, one of them keeps trying to get into the fish pond and they're both digging holes to China through my lawn. This one chews chair legs and she has already chewed her bed basket to shreds. Please. Help!"

For each new client I fill out a *Dog Behavioral Profile* form, which is like a patient's medical chart at a hospital. It enables everyone who works with the dog to be aware of the personality type and behavioral problems, and the dog's progress is then entered on a blank training sheet. Looking at the chart for the McMahon dogs I could see that they were playful, responsive, and affectionate and, at times, stubborn and slightly aggressive. What he wanted most out of the training program, according to a note on the form, was for the dogs to obey him. At first I gave the two young dogs six lessons at home. The next step was training them in our kennel for fourteen weeks. That was where they became socialized and learned to adjust to all kinds of new people and new situations. The dogs at the kennel were handled by many different people—more than thirty employees—over a long period of time, which made them adaptive to most people and eager to learn.

On the three occasions that Ed came to the kennel to visit the dogs he arrived in a chauffeur-driven stretch limo. I suspect that he doesn't like to drive cars, despite the fact that he was a jet pilot in the Marine Corps. His visits were a great occasion for everyone at the kennel. He was happy with what we were doing with his dogs and he made everyone feel appreciated for their work. Ed is a large, robust man, full of life, friendly, caring, and happy-go-lucky. The thing about Ed McMahon is that when he talks to you he makes you feel like he's known you for at least a hundred years. Considering his line of work it should come as no surprise that he's a very funny man with the ability to make you feel good.

He cared a lot about his dogs. On each of his visits he spent at least one hour playing with them, talking to them, finding out about their progress, and learning what his responsibilities were for the future. The kennel training lasted several months, but the animals responded well to it and went home as better-behaved dogs than when they arrived. All I can say about Ed McMahon is that it was as much fun training his dogs as it was working with him on "The Tonight Show."

When you're in the middle of writing a book titled *Woof!* and a woman calls and asks you to train her dogs, one of whom is named Woof, you just scratch your head and smile, especially if that woman is Whoopi Goldberg. On a Saturday morning in May 1993, while I was in the middle of my Saturday circus, I was called to the phone. Someone from the office said she thought it was Whoopi Goldberg.

"Oh, sure. Right. Whoopi Goldberg has nothing better to do than call *me* at eight in the morning," I answered sarcastically. People on my staff were always joking around like that. However, I stopped what I was doing and took the call so that I wouldn't be thought rude by a possible client.

"Hello," I said in an impatient manner.

"Matthew?"

"Yes."

"Whoopi Goldberg."

"Hi," I answered with an embarrassed smile on my face. It really was her. You couldn't mistake her distinctive, gravelly voice. There is just no way of being prepared for a moment like that. I tried to sound unimpressed but I am not a cool person and my sappy enthusiasm uncontrollably bubbles up. She told me that she was looking through the Yellow Pages and enjoyed my ad with a picture of a Dalmatian kissing my ear and thought it was a real loving thing. She had just gotten two Rhodesian Ridgeback puppies the night before. They were peeing and potting all over her place and made her realize that they were not something she could handle by herself.

"I'm acting fast," she said with a laugh. "I need help."

I explained to her about my program and that I would love to see the dogs right away in order to evaluate them. She explained that she was going to perform at a benefit show that night in San Diego. I suggested that she bring the dogs to my kennel on her way out of town. It was the only way I could get on the case as fast as she wanted me to. She agreed and thought it was a good idea.

At eleven o'clock that morning Whoopi arrived at the kennel in a large limo with a driver, followed by a van with the two puppies in it being driven by her brother. Her plan was to talk to me, have the dogs evaluated, sign a contract for the training, and continue on to San Diego in her limo while her brother drove the dogs back to her house. She arrived during my busiest time of the week. It is when I do most of the evaluations of new dogs while my trainers teach their resident canine students all over the place. Additionally, there are many clients in and out, visiting their dogs. As you can imagine, the arrival of Whoopi Goldberg's caravan attracted quite a bit of attention.

I greeted her as she stepped out of her car and introduced myself. It's funny: You never know what to expect. What surprised me about her was that there were no surprises. Whoopi is Whoopi. There is no difference in her appearance or personality on or off the stage. She is a very funny, very real person with no airs about her.

"Matthew, you know, we've got to do something here," she said comically in her deep, raspy voice. "We've got to get these dogs under control before they ruin my life. The dogs gotta learn to be good puppies." Although she was smiling that famous broad grin of hers, she really needed help. I've seen the look thousands of times. She wanted to do the right thing and didn't mind making the effort. I evaluated her two dogs and saw right away that they were very sweet, very affectionate puppies. She had not been able to get them to accept wearing a leash and collar and didn't know how to handle that problem. The first thing I did was leash-break the two of them so that they could be brought under control right away. Within twenty minutes I was able to get them to walk on a leash. It made a good impression on her. The dogs did very well that morning.

"Okay," she said, "let's get this thing done." She signed a contract and I set up a temporary housebreaking schedule for the puppies. We made an appointment for me to go to her house the next morning, after she returned from San Diego, to set up a permanent training program. Before she left I gave her two dog crates so that she could confine the puppies to a specific area of her house. After we concluded our business she got in her limo and drove off in one direction as her brother took the puppies into the van and drove off in the opposite direction.

The next morning, Sunday, I was at her house in Pacific Palisades at nine sharp. Even though she did not get back from her concert until two in the morning she was up and waiting for me, full of energy and raring to go. I gave her a complete

Although I had met Betty White on a number of occasions,
it was a joy to be sharing just a bit of her spotlight.

housebreaking schedule, walked around her lovely home, and advised her where to keep the dogs so they wouldn't ruin it. One puppy's name was Sam and the other was named Woof, and I advised Whoopi that it was important to begin a bonding process with each dog so that a relationship develops. I then worked with each dog for about half an hour and set up a training schedule, which began on Monday, the very next day.

I arrived at her house as promised, at seven in the morning, and found her out on the street in a great, funny old hat, walking her two dogs and cleaning up after them with paper towels like everyone else. She is one hell of a great dog owner. What I loved about her is how she took care of the animals. She had these two big bowls and I watched her feed the dogs: first one, waiting for him to finish, then the other. Although she had a lot of help around the house she did almost everything for them herself. When the dogs had "accidents" she was the one who cleaned them up. Her interest in her dogs was touching. She was very affectionate with them and held them, hugged them, and talked to them. When we discussed housebreaking I told her that odor neutralizers were a very important part of the procedure. I explained that you had to get rid of the odors from the places where the dogs had their "accidents"—otherwise they would keep going back to eliminate on those same spots. It was a matter of claiming territory. I told her about several commercially prepared products available that are designed for that specific purpose.

Her eyes squinted and that devilish smile of hers spread across her face. She said, "Now you see, I just instinctively knew that you're supposed to do that. You know what I've been using to get rid of the smell?"

"What?"

"Balsamic vinegar."

And she meant it. For three days she had been scrubbing the floor where the dogs let loose with expensive balsamic vinegar, a gourmet condiment.

"You know, Whoopi," I said, "I wondered why your house smells like salad. You've given a whole new meaning to balsamic vinegar. I'll probably never have a salad again."

There are some celebrities that are regarded by everyone as living legends and seem to all of us to be bigger than life. When you meet them with their dogs, though, you share a common ground that cuts through all of that and helps you see them as real people. That was certainly the case with Jimmy Stewart and his wife, Gloria.

I first met the Stewarts at a book signing in the Neiman-

Marcus store in Beverly Hills on a Saturday afternoon in March 1991. They were there with Betty White, and Leslie Charleson of the TV soap opera "General Hospital," and me, to autograph copies of a beautiful, coffee-table book we were portrayed in along with many other celebrity dog lovers. The book was called *Top Dog*, published by Beautiful America, and I was the only dog trainer in the collection of notable dog owners. All the others were very famous people. Although I had met Betty White on a number of occasions it was a joy to be sharing just a bit of her spotlight. She is, without a doubt, the funniest woman on television, but more than that, a great animal person. More people have become kinder to animals in this country because of Betty White than anyone else I can think of. We began signing books almost the moment we entered the store.

The Stewarts quietly walked in half an hour later and made the occasion even more memorable than I thought it could be. There were many ooos and aaahs and a bit of applause from the crowd of people who had gathered to see the celebrities. He smiled and waved to everyone, sat down at a table next to a stack of books, and began autographing them for people. There were between fifty and a hundred people present in addition to many members of the TV and print media. James Stewart was living history to me and there we were, standing next to each other, signing the same book. I was excited by the prospect of meeting him and his wife, Gloria.

I couldn't resist having my picture taken with him and asking him to sign my personal copy of the book. Age has slowed Mr. Stewart down and made him somewhat fragile. He was quite reserved and moved carefully, although he was very nice and pleasant to be with. By contrast, Gloria was energetic, flamboyant, articulate, and quite outspoken. We struck up a conversation about dogs while her husband signed books for the eager people lined up for his autograph. When she found out that I was a trainer she started talking about her own dogs, as many people do after meeting me. She told me they had two Golden Retrievers and that her daughter had recently found a stray dog they named Princess, a mixed breed, which they took off her hands. They gave the dog a home with them and were trying to deal with some of her behavior problems. I told her that I would send her copies of *Good Dog, Bad Dog* and *When Good Dogs Do Bad Things*, where she was sure to find some help. It was a thrill to be able to send Mr. and Mrs. James Stewart copies of my books.

I sent the books to them by messenger the following Monday, hoping they would like them. About two weeks later Gloria Stewart called me at my office and asked me to train her dogs. I tried not to sound childish, so I jumped for joy in silence as I explained to her about training in the home as opposed to training in the kennel, which involved keeping the dogs with me for a length of time.

She answered, "Oh, no. I couldn't leave my dogs in a kennel. What would I do without them?"

I said, "Well, it would be like sending them to camp."

She replied, "*My* house is camp."

The more she told me about the dogs, the more they sounded shy to me and needful of the kind of socializing we do best at the kennel. I finally convinced her that the kennel was the best way to handle the problems. I had the dogs picked up from their home in Beverly Hills on a Friday. The next day she called me.

"Matthew, send the dogs home. We can't deal with their absence."

I brought the dogs back to her that day and set up a schedule of training sessions in their home that would take several months. After a while it became clear to them that the dogs' shyness necessitated their being trained at the kennel. There was no other way to bring about the changes they wanted. She and Mr. Stewart didn't like the idea of all three of them gone at one time but maybe two was all right. So two dogs were brought to the kennel and one stayed at home. Later I had to bring the third one in to complete the training and that set in motion a string of phone calls from Mrs. Stewart.

"How are they?"

"They are probably lonely."

"They probably need me."

My answer was always the same. "I know they need you, but they need to be trained, Mrs. Stewart."

The Stewart Golden Retrievers, Kelly and Judy.

*The dogs kept going back and forth from my kennel to
the magnificent Stewart home in Beverly Hills, where I
did my best to train them and their owners.*

"Oh, call me Gloria, Matthew."

Somehow I couldn't bring myself to call her anything but Mrs. Stewart, even when she would verbally duel with me.

"My dogs are not so bad. Matthew, you know they're not so bad."

I would answer her with great patience, "Well, then why did you send them in?"

She would reply, "They had a little problem but... they're not so bad!"

It was very touching. The Stewarts without their dogs were like flowers without rain. They needed them. Their dogs were a very important part of their lives and parting with them, even for a short time, was hard. They came out to visit them one Saturday, naturally, in the middle of the usual Saturday glut of trainers and clients. There were many hushed murmurs of, "Oh, my God, it's Jimmy Stewart," and practically everything came to a halt.

James Stewart is a quiet, charming man who handles the adulation of his admirers with warm, generous appreciation. He shook the hand of everyone there who offered it and said hello to all of them in the most pleasant, becoming way. Both he and Mrs. Stewart seemed pleased at the way we were bringing their dogs around and, of course, they were very happy to see them.

Before they left she looked at me and said, "I don't like this. I want my dogs home."

I threw my arms in the air and had no choice but to comply. The dogs went back and forth from the kennel to the Stewarts' home several times after that. I found myself training the two Goldens in the magnificent Stewart home in Beverly Hills while I kept Princess in the kennel. In the course of this period of the training Mrs. Stewart told me that the biggest problem was that the dogs jumped on her. I taught her how to administer a corrective jerk with the leash whenever the dogs jumped, but she didn't want to do it. When they jumped on her she would tell them how nice they were, which was, in effect, rewarding them for it. She was always complaining about the dogs barking, jumping, and pulling, and how they didn't listen to her. But when I showed her what to do she would ask, "Do I have to correct them?" She wanted well-trained dogs without being a well-trained trainer. I started calling her a wuss with her dogs, the ultimate dog mommy.

Finally, I returned Princess to their home and took the two Goldens back to the kennel to finish up their training. She said it was okay.

"I have to have at least one dog home. I can't do this anymore. I don't sleep. It's awful for me."

Well, the Stewarts are finally reunited with all their dogs and they are better-behaved than they were, but there were times when I thought we'd never get the training completed. I can't believe it's over. Somehow I think the saga will continue. We'll see. Although James Stewart is not a man of many words, as most of his millions of fans know, it is obvious to anyone who knows them that he and Gloria love their dogs almost as much as they love each other, and that's saying a lot. They are two of the most gracious people I have ever met in my life.

Throughout the years in Los Angeles I have been asked many times to participate in activities that improved the lives of many people by helping them make closer contact with dogs. For example, I have given a great deal of my time to the Los Angeles Society for the Prevention of Cruelty to Animals and to the Los Angeles County Shelter for Abused and Disadvantaged Children at Maclaren Hall. Bringing troubled kids and dogs together for the first time in a positive, wholesome way is one of the most important things I have ever done, and has given me great pride and satisfaction in what I do for a living. I am also a Reserve Animal Control Officer for the Los Angeles Department of Animal Regulation and sit on the Licensing Committee for Sentry Dog Operators. All of these activities are strictly voluntary; they are simply a way of putting something back in the pot and saying thanks for everything.

One of the more interesting contributions made to the community was the vocational program in dog training I set up at the California Institution for Women at Frontera, more commonly known as Chino, a prison for women. The pilot program, under the auspices of the Delta Society, helped six women complete a sixteen-week, state-accredited vocational rehabilitation course in dog training. For four months my assistant and I drove from Monterey Park to Frontera every Tuesday and Thursday morning with three German Shepherds—Candy, Tippy, and my own beloved Emily—and a little Maltese named Ralph for my imprisoned students to work with. Talk about a captive audience. I'll never forget that graduation day back in 1985 as long as I live. One of the women, who became a pretty fair dog trainer and, I hope, no longer an inmate, said it all when she simply stated, "If the dogs think I'm okay, I must not be too bad."

In 1986 I volunteered to be part of a dog obedience program with the Beverly Hills Municipal Court, which involved telephone and on-site counseling for people with unruly pets. As a result of that involvement I was asked by Los Angeles City

Attorney James K. Hahn to be part of the nation's first Canine Court, a program designed to divert public nuisance cases involving unruly dogs from the overloaded court system and counsel owners how to control their pets. It was a way of taking almost two thousand animal-related cases a year out of the regular court system, which cost the city $100,000 a year, and giving them special attention of a more positive nature.

The plaintiffs and the defendants were requested to appear before me and state their cases, and I would try to arbitrate them not so much as a judge but as a counselor. Although I functioned as a hearing officer, I was able to ask questions that judges just didn't have the knowledge to ask. I was able to bridge the communication gap between dogs and people. Part of my duty as "doggy judge" was to help resolve each case with helpful advice for dog owners and those making complaints about dogs. With few exceptions, most of the cases I heard involved dogs that barked excessively, driving their neighbors crazy. When one defendant said he kept his barking dogs outside at night because they messed in the house while he slept, I helped him set up a housebreaking program. In every city in America, the dog wars go on because people do not know how to get their pets under control. Far too many pet owners live with their dogs' behavior problems and expect everyone else to do the same. Having a "love me, love my dog" attitude often lands you in court answering a civil complaint that can be costly.

Canine Court was the nation's first private mediation service devoted exclusively to canine-related disputes, and emotions there ran high when we were in session. As far as I could tell, it was the people who drove the dogs crazy, not the other way around. I very often found myself speaking on behalf of

NIDT director of training, Sherry Davis, "socializing" a friend. Some dog problems, such as shyness, aggressiveness toward other dogs, and aggressiveness toward people, are dealt with more effectively at the kennel than at home.

the dog and stating the case for him. Most of the cases were easily resolved by showing the dog owners how to keep their dogs problem-free. If you can stop a destructive chewing problem, for example, then you can allow your dog to stay indoors, and effectively solve his all-night barking problem. Based on the public and media response, Canine Court was a howling success.

Someone once referred to my training kennel in Monterey Park as the Betty Ford Treatment Center for the Rehabilitation of Dogs. Of course, the dogs that come here do not suffer from substance abuse, unless you consider love, affection, and lots of attention to be addictive. I don't believe a dog can get too much of that. When I first started I only trained dogs in the home. I considered that to be the best place to do it because problems such as housebreaking, chewing, and all the rest were in the home and that's where you had to deal with them. It is also an important opportunity to work with the dog owners as well. Once I started working in my own kennel I realized that some of the problems, such as shyness, aggressiveness toward other dogs, or aggressiveness toward people, couldn't be dealt with as effectively in the home.

I now understand that it is better to match the environment to the problem. If the dog is having a home problem, that's where it should be dealt with. Although training in both environments works, sometimes one is better than the other. For example, you should not train a dog in a kennel until it is at least six months old. Young puppies *must* be trained in the home because that's where the initial problems are and that's where the bonding between a dog and its family must take place. When people have dog problems that cannot be resolved in the home or when they don't have time to put in the work then they must send the dog to a training kennel. The learning process for dogs involves a great deal of practice and repetition of what the dog has been taught. All the dog training in the world is useless if the dog owners do not put in the necessary practice, and that's where kennel training helps. Working in my own kennel has enabled me to solve some of the most difficult behavior and personality problems in dogs that I could never have helped otherwise. Some of the dogs that are left with me are dangerous when they come in and completely controllable when they leave. Such was the case with Gerde, my permanent guest.

Back in 1985 the Darlingtons used to show up at the kennel every Saturday to see Gerde, their German Shepherd, who was a big, fifteen-month-old dog. He was more dog than they had bargained for and they just couldn't handle him. He growled at everyone, jumped at people, and pulled hard on the leash when he wanted his way, which was all the time. Gerde was growing into a huge, dangerous dog. The elderly couple had seen me on a local television show and just showed up at the kennel one day asking if I could do something with this unmanageable dog of theirs.

I evaluated the brutish animal with a lump in my throat until I worked with him for a few minutes. He was a dominant-aggressive dog with a keen intelligence and a hidden sweetness that is hard to explain considering his frightening behavior, especially toward strangers. Gerde was a dog person's dog. He was completely devoted to those in his life, but he was very much their leader as far as he was concerned. The dog controlled his domain with flashing teeth and ferocious growling. If you looked into his intense eyes you knew you were in trouble. He was like a domineering father who was always hollering at his family, but one who would give his life for them. Gerde was not meant to be someone's pet. He was, in every sense, the original dog, a leader of dogs.

Mrs. Darlington explained that they had acquired him more for companionship than protection and had come to love him very much. Gerde was, however, beyond their ability to handle. It was a rare challenge to work with a dog like that and get him to accept control from a couple that were obviously frail and breakable. The dog had completely captivated me and I decided to take him on. I trained him myself for three months and was pleased with his progress. He was tough as nails but he did wonderfully. Although he knew I was not afraid of him he also understood that I had great respect for him. Once I got him under control, the next step, probably the most difficult part, was to transfer control from me to the elderly couple.

Mr. and Mrs. Darlington by then had become more than clients. They had become friends, and I began to look forward to their Saturday visits. Mr. Darlington was in his late seventies and his sweet wife was just a bit younger. They were like doting grandparents to me who were more interested in the younger people around them than in themselves. Mrs. Darlington, a heavyset woman, loved to bring large amounts of her cooking with her each Saturday. Most of the clients who came on Saturday brought food for their dogs but she also brought food, lots of it, for everyone. Her casseroles and cakes and salads were pure Americana, and we enjoyed her cooking very much. Mr. Darlington was gentle, kind, and genuinely interested in other people. They were both very reassuring people who believed in their own optimism. They were a loving couple, growing old together, representing what we all were taught that marriage was supposed to be.

Like so many others, they thought of their Saturday visits as a combination social event and support group meeting. Among those they befriended were another elderly couple, Ted and Marlin Seldes, whose Doberman had been kidnapped and left in the trunk of a car for twenty-four hours. The dog was almost dead when the police found her and the experience had so profoundly frightened her that she bit anyone that went near her. I was working hard on that Dobie to restore her self-confidence and make her comfortable around humans once again. The two couples had found each other at the kennel and had become close friends because of their shared feelings for their dogs.

On the thirteenth or fourteenth week of their involvement with me, the Darlingtons did not show up for the Saturday visit and didn't call either. It was not at all like them. The following Wednesday, I called them at home only to learn the sad news that Mr. Darlington had passed away. We sent flowers and several of us, including myself, attended the funeral. It was a sad event for all of us. The following week Mrs. Darlington came to the kennel to visit Gerde by herself. Naturally, we all tried to give her as much attention as we thought she should have. She smiled gratefully and took great comfort from seeing how well her dog was doing. The dog, of course, was pleased to see her and was working well with her. She would walk him around on-leash and he would accept her commands to Heel and to Sit. That pleased me a lot.

I looked forward to seeing her on the following Saturday to teach her to place Gerde in the Down position, which is the most difficult command to get a dog to accept. The entire day

Gerde.

went by but she never came. This time I called at the end of the day only to learn from her brother that she too had passed away. There were tears and genuine expressions of loss from many of us who knew her. It was a depressing time. Later that week Mrs. Darlington's brother called me. He informed me that his sister had added a paragraph to her will the week before, leaving Gerde to me because she knew how much I loved him. I swore to him and to myself that I would always take good care of him. She gave me her most treasured possession to care for and I felt deeply honored and very touched by it. Whenever I see Gerde sitting up in his spacious dog run we look into each other's eyes and I say to him, "I know. I miss them too."

It was late June 1990, on a typically busy Saturday at the kennel in Monterey Park. My stomach was telling me that I had missed lunch as I sat in my office listening to a psychotherapist whose dog I was training. The woman was not happy with my work. Evidently she thought it was psychologically damaging to expect her to take a leadership position over her dog. She then carefully explained to me why my training techniques were all wrong for her and her dog and began to conduct a seminar on what I should be doing with all dogs everywhere.

"Do you really see patients?" I asked. "I mean, do people actually come to you for help?"

Cars were pulling in and pulling out of our driveway and the rush of people visiting their dogs was in full swing as six or seven trainers were working their canine students in what space was available. The phones were ringing, the fax machine was tweaking, and even the coffeemaker was gurgling a loud, bubbly noise as a continuously running tape of my "Today Show" interview with Bryant Gumble played overhead on a TV screen mounted on the wall. The joint was jumping. I excused myself when my client started quoting from the Sermon on the Mount and how it pertained to dogs. I slipped out of the office for a cup of coffee.

As I took a third sip I suddenly heard a group of people start to sing an enthusiastic but off-key rendition of "Happy Birthday." It was coming from the patio.

> "Happy Birthday to you.
> Happy Birthday to you.
> Happy Birthday, dear Bagel,
> Happy Birthday to you."

A cheer went up and the sound of many people applauding filled the air. I ran outside, around the front, through the wooden gate, and into the shady patio to see what the commotion was all about. To my amazement all I could see at first were hundreds of red, green, and white balloons hanging from the trees and bushes; long ones, round ones, big ones, little ones. They were all over the place. At the picnic table under the big tree were Doris Longella and her Beagle along with many of the visiting clients and members of my staff who should have been working. They were all wearing shiny colored party hats—you know, the dunce hats with a rubber band that goes under the chin.

In the center of the table were two very large birthday cakes. One was a two-layered affair with gobs of white buttercream and red and green curly trim around the edge with writing scrawled across the top. The other cake, upon close examination, had a hardened white coating over several layers of chopped liver. Everyone was having a good time singing, chatting, laughing, and eating cake. It was not a good idea to say something that might possibly introduce a negative feeling to the affair. In the center of it all was Miss Longella, holding her young Beagle and hugging him. Several of my other clients were holding their dogs in much the same way and having a good time. I peeked over at the cake to see what was written on it.

It said, "Happy Bow-Wow Day to Bagel the Beagle. One Year Old." It seemed like a lot of writing for someone that can't read. I saw the woman who is my director of training and motioned to her. She tried to duck away but I called out her name.

"What's going on?" I asked.

"Oh, Matt," she answered with impatience. "It's Bagel's first birthday and Doris asked if it was okay to give him a party since he was spending it here. I didn't want to bother you with small details."

"Small details? In the middle of the busiest day of the week we're holding a birthday party for a dog and you didn't want to bother me with the details?"

Suddenly from out front a series of car horns started honking away, cutting through the noise of Bagel's party. Now I have seen many long processions of cars going into the cemetery across the road; that happens all the time out here. But I had never heard them honking like that before, as though they were throwing some dead guy a big sendoff. My head trainer grabbed my arm as I was about to run out front.

"Oh," she said. "That's probably the wedding party."

I shook my head and asked, "What wedding party?"

"There are a number of little things I do for clients that make them happy. This is one of them. We're training two dogs for Susan Poole and her fiancé, Phil Arends."

"Uh-huh," I said with what little patience I had left.

"They got married today and their two dogs are really important to them and they want to be photographed with the dogs in their wedding outfits."

"How did I lose control here? I mean, when did it happen?" I asked.

"Matt," she said, "the dogs are here being trained. How else are they going to get the picture they want?" With that she walked away trying to catch up with the happy couple.

I returned to the office and watched what was going on from the window. It was around two in the afternoon and a particularly hot day. There were several cars, with pink and white streamers hanging from their sides. The lead car was a big London taxi, all black and boxy, with a uniformed driver in the front seat. It even had the steering wheel on the right side. The driver hopped out, opened the rear door and out stepped a young couple in full formal wedding attire, smiling from ear to ear. The groom was dressed in a white tuxedo jacket over black trousers and the bride wore a full-train wedding gown with a long lace veil and sumptuous white puffs of satin and lace wherever you looked. As befuddled as I was about the whole thing it was obvious that they were excited, happy, and great-looking. With one hand holding the veil on top of her head and the other pulling the bottom of the train off the grass, she and her new husband marched up the crushed pebble incline toward the office. Mrs. Arends, the former Susan Poole, flung open the door and said to the receptionist, "We'd like to see Ben and Lucky, please."

I walked over to them, chuckled, and said, "I get it. This is a joke, right? It's another gag that the staff is pulling on me."

Susan smiled and said, "Matthew, I'd like you to meet my . . . ahem, husband, Phil."

I looked at them both and finally started to believe it.

"Why? Why are you doing this?" I asked.

Susan smiled and said, "These dogs are a big part of our lives. They are the reason we got together."

Phil joined in. "We were both working at the same travel agency on the campus at Cal State in Los Angeles. I ran the agency. To tell the truth, I didn't think it was a good idea to get involved with an employee. But I saw her in the park one afternoon with her beautiful Samoyed, Ben, and we started talking. I found out that she was totally caught up in this an-

woof!

*"Since Ben and Lucky are a big part of this wedding, the day would
not be complete without having them in a picture with us," Susan said.*

208

imal. Every penny she earned went into this unruly dog and that impressed me.''

"Why?" I asked.

"Well," he answered, "I was with my dog, too, and discovered that we both loved dogs with a passion. It changed everything and all the rules went out the window."

I smiled and said, "Oh, I remember. You own Lucky, the German Shepherd mix, and Susan owns the Samoyed."

"Right," said Susan. "If it hadn't been for them we might never have gotten together. Look, Matt, we just got married in the church that my grandfather designed and it's a wonderful time for us, loaded with good feelings about family and everything. We've had formal portraits taken with all our family members at the church and at the reception at home. Since Ben and Lucky are a big part of this wedding, the day would not be complete without having them in a picture with us."

By then several kennel workers had retrieved the two dogs and everyone assembled out on the grass in front of the office. The bride, the groom, and the four-legged matchmakers stood alone and smiled for the camera. It was fun watching them pose with their dogs. You couldn't help sharing their pleasure. Some of us—I will not name names—got a little wet in the eyes. After they shot half a roll of film, Susan and Phil hugged their dogs, said good-bye to everyone, and got inside their London taxi. Phil pulled a large, wet bottle out of a metal ice bucket and poured two glasses of champagne, handing one to his beautiful bride. They toasted their glasses and waved to everyone as they drove off to their honeymoon. I wondered if tears come out of white satin and lace. I wondered if they should.

I knew that someday Phil and Susan's children were going

to make them tell the story of their wedding day over and over again, and how the love of their dogs brought them together. What a victory it was for them. It gave me pleasure just to be a small part of it.

You have to smile when you think about how many great stories there are about people whose lives were changed because of dogs. That's my story. When I was a young man I was unhappy because I wanted something more than what seemed available. I blindly tried to go out on my own but it didn't take long to get lost along the way. Taking charge of your own life is risky business and can be a painful road to follow. I did it anyway, and I'm glad I did, but I took some lumps. Still, I knew I was headed in the right direction the moment I decided to

Every Saturday, dozens of nervous, anxiety-ridden people show up loaded with gifts for their dogs. It's a good thing dogs don't laugh.

work with dogs. In the beginning, it was Silver and me out there together growing up and trying to find a little piece of the world to fit into. Since then, there have been many dogs and many people in my life, but mostly dogs. What more could I want? That's been my victory.

The day was winding down and everyone was heading for a cool, quiet place, to get out of the sun. Our visitors had already gone home and I couldn't help thinking about birthdays and weddings and dogs. My mind drifted as it occasionally does to a place where I could think about all the dogs I ever knew and all the people I got to know because of them. I went back to work and I felt good.

Here's to *your* victory.

acknowledgments

Beverly Margolis—Without your love, help, support, and courage, I would never have been able to achieve the successes I've had. There are no words to describe someone who is so loving and giving. You are just as beautiful inside as you are outside.

Jesse Margolis—My dearest son, whose love of his dog, Emily, was so beautiful to watch and to be a part of.

Dave and Rhea Margolis—my mom and dad—and my wonderful, loving sister, Eila. The dogs brought us together.

Alan Feinstein—As a child and as an adult, I have placed the highest value on our friendship. You have always been there for me. Nothing in this book would have happened if it hadn't been for you, my dear friend, and I will always be there for you.

Mordecai Siegal—You are the brother that I never had and always wanted, with all the fighting, making up, and loving that goes with that special relationship. If it wasn't for your professionalism and your caring friendship, my career, such as it is, would not exist. You took my knowledge, added your own, and transformed it into readable, entertaining, useful information. Without you there would be no words.

Vicki Siegal—Special thanks and gratitude for all your help. You have worked tirelessly on our books over the years, and I know you never allow a manuscript to leave the house until you are satisfied with it. You have been a good friend for a long time.

Jay Collins—The kindest and most professional man I have ever met. You taught me so much about myself and my professional life, all in such a positive way. I'll always cherish your involvement.

Sherry Davis—One of the most knowledgeable and dedicated dog trainers I've ever had the pleasure of working with. No one can take better care of the dogs than you.

Janell Wilson—Your love of dogs and dedication to the job goes far beyond what any employer could hope for. I'm so proud of you.

Captain Arthur J. Haggerty—How fortunate I was to learn from the very best.

Michael Hartig—If it wasn't for you, I wouldn't have found me.

Michael Zannella—Thanks for making that incredibly important phone call to Bob Dolce and for having faith in me.

Bob Dolce—Thank you for the opportunity to be a guest on "The Tonight Show (Starring Johnny Carson)."

Eileen Blake—Thank God for your patience and caring.

Karen Golay—You surely made me look good on TV. Please don't show anyone the outtakes.

Federation Employment Guidance Service (United Jewish Appeal-Federation of Jewish Philanthropies)—With heartfelt gratitude for providing me with the Interest-Aptitude Value Test, which

Rg==

Rw==

SA==

SQ==

Sg==

Sw==

TA==

TQ==

Tg==

Tw==

UA==

UQ==

Ug==

Uw==

VA==

VQ==

Vg==

Vw==

WA==

WQ==

Wg==

acknowledgments

changed my life in such an important way. A special thank you to my counselor, Robert Lipton, and to his successor, Barry Lustig.

Jimmy and Gloria Stewart—A special thanks for trusting me with your most precious possessions. You win the prize for babying your dogs. You were very kind.

Mary Tondorf-Dick—Thank you so much for conceiving the idea of this book.

Helene Steel—What a friend! Thank you for generously adding your most competent photographs.

To the people and dogs in the photos— Your presence on these pages has added so much. With gratitude to: Sherry Davis, NIDT trainer; Robert Pirro, NIDT trainer; Christina Rothenhausler, NIDT trainer; Jeff Brake, NIDT trainer; Sandy and Nancy Bressler with Calvin (Wheaten Terrier); Lydia and Kevin Bartlett with Nikita (Akita); Renee and Donna Albertson with Lucy (Golden Retriever); Merilyn and Jerry Tripp with Buffy (Maltese); Silver (Weimaraner); Captain Haggerty with two friends, Pete (Siberian Husky) and Princess (Maltese); Jimmy Stewart with Kelly and Judy Stewart (Golden Retrievers); Gerde (German Shepherd Dog); Betty White; Susan and Phil Arends (the bride and groom) with Ben and Lucky (Samoyed and German Shepherd Dog mix).

And finally, to all the dogs in my life whom I have loved with all my heart, among them are: Smoky, Silver, Princess, Emily, Quint, Ulli, Tillie, Pete, Winner, Bruce, and, of course, Tim . . . *Woof!*